TESSELLATIONS

TESSELLATIONS

Patterns of Life and Death in the Company of a Master

LUCY OLIVER

Matador
9 Priory Business Park,
Wistow Road, Kibworth Beauchamp,
Leicestershire. LE8 0RX
Tel: 0116 279 2299
Email: books@troubador.co.uk
Web: www.troubador.co.uk/matador
Twitter: @matadorbooks

ISBN 978 183859 294 3

British Library Cataloguing in Publication Data.
A catalogue record for this book is available from the British Library.

Cover illustration: Tessellation by Michael Frenda

Printed and bound in the UK by TJ International, Padstow, Cornwall
Typeset in 11pt Adobe Garamond Pro by Troubador Publishing Ltd, Leicester, UK

Matador is an imprint of Troubador Publishing Ltd

MIX
Paper from responsible sources
FSC® C013056

In dedication to the long lineage of the Common Life.

Contents

Preface

This is a book for core seekers.
The illustrations and incidents of an ordinary life and a non-ordinary life are teaching cores.
Read fast, it will entertain.
Read slowly, the seeds of knowing will take root.
Take your time.

Introduction

It was in late 1970's London that I first heard I heard a voice from the darkness[1]. I didn't know it then, but it was a voice springing from an oral tradition of Knowledge which has run like a thread through the religious history of the West, surfacing here and there, sometimes in a conventionally religious setting, but in our age no longer needing to shelter in any particular religious context.

Hearing that voice initiated for me a metaphysical, spiritual and esoteric journey, 'esoteric' in the sense of 'inner', deeply veiled and needing to be revealed. My account of that training is personal—glimpses through the veils—but the glimpses will contain as much information as I can insert about the path I have followed, with others, under the tutelage of a wise and remarkable man, our Psychopomp (guide of souls). We simply called him Glyn.

Glyn's teaching and formulations were resolutely based on *first principles*, the simplicity at the root of phenomena, and on number, which is a lineage dating at least from Pythagoras. To those who could see it, he was a Man of Knowledge, but he was determined to be anonymous, and discouraged any seeds of incipient guru worship. There are few photos of him at any age, and he lived a reclusive existence in a West London flat until his death at the age of 78. I thought I had a photo containing a small figure at the edge of one of our public Turning performances, but when I dug the photos out and pored over with a magnifying glass after his death, either that particular photo had slipped between the worlds, or he had faded himself off the film surface!

The lineage has its roots way back in the West; the transmission oral—that is, from person to person, an interaction and communication through living fields of being. An interesting question for a digital age is to ask how relevant is person-to-person oral transmission when you can have a super-abundance of teachings delivered right to your favourite arm-chair with a mere touch of the finger-tips? What factors make mere words *connect*? What can protect a seeker from plunging into a sea of information and accumulating a spiritual junk-heap consisting of the best bits of every teaching? What *methods or tools* are needed to forge a soul from this junk-yard of Infinity? With what *faculty* does one recognize Truth, or sift gold from psychological debris?

The spirit, we are told, hovers over the Deep. But can personal 'fields' of being interact through screens? How can the kind of contact controlled by the flick of a button be rooted in a deep level of Field, of the kind which facilitates 'transmission' of truth? These are new questions, new avenues to be explored, tested and validated. We are at the beginning of a new spiritual epoch.

But what is meant by 'spiritual'? Nowadays it covers all kinds of technologically and pharmacologically assisted experimentation and aspiration, divorced from any 'religious' background. A thoughtful person might say "I'm not a religious person, but I am spiritual", and a declared secular or agnostic thinker may use traditionally spiritual practices like meditation purely to assist thinking with clarity and focus, or for the emotional rewards. Many of the teachings which are easily available and called 'spiritual', are essentially about health, therapy, or self-development. The boundaries have become blurred, so it is timely to see if there are root principles which will open up the true depths in any formulation.

The path presented in this book begins with a portrait of the man whose grasp of the Reality I sought to know was beyond anything I had encountered before or have encountered since. He weaves in and out of this account as my view of a being I could not entirely comprehend. There were aspects through which Glyn related to others which were strange to me, and I have not done justice to those Glyns. I knew I could not get his measure, and was often puzzled and slightly awed in the presence of interactions and atmospheres which were bypassing me, even as I sat there and tried to take part. However, I hope that the Glyn of this narrative would be recognisable as an accurate portrayal by those who took part in the collective activities which he initiated over nearly forty years.

The second element in my narrative is the collective background of individuals who came together for so many years to study, formulate and grow with a common purpose, namely, to be educated in all aspects of developing Knowledge and Being. An esoteric education implied de-cluttering essential principle from the padding of millennia formed by custom, interpretation and ethnic accretions, and had to include clear structured thinking as well as emotional understanding, self-discipline, and grounding in the body and in everyday life.

Our training began under Glyn's idiosyncratic direction, but he was determined that we were all individuals and all equal; there was to be no group-think or moulding to fit some ideal. Inevitably, unavoidably perhaps, this in itself became a moulding, which succeeded only too well. "You're all Bigheads," he'd say. We took this as a term of endearment—precisely proving the point! But at the same time, anyone who appeared to be gaining personal power or authority would likely be referred to in his conversation as "Old Buggerlugs there", as if, just at that moment, the name was escaping him... .

The accounts which make up the bulk of this book began life as a long-running correspondence between myself and Alice, a friend who had re-located to Washington DC. She had never met the subject of these memoirs, the person of Glyn, but had absorbed something of the teaching and methodology he established, and incorporated this particular kind of inner work into her life. Always eager for more detail, she would generate emails and questions. I have taken these as the basis for the elaboration which follows.

Hence the format is thematic, and meanders between three elements woven into a narrative: firstly, the inspirational figure of Glyn as initiator and fount of formulation; intertwined with the second strand, the community of work, philosophy and theory which developed under his guidance; and a necessary third element, which is something of my own story.

Like the other two threads my presence in the narrative is meant to be illustrative, and though necessarily filtered through my particular psyche and motivation, I try to anchor events in a time and place and to describe the circumstances as faithfully as possible. Fundamentally, it is all an Abstract from life—like any re-telling, like memory itself—an abstract from the living reality of experience in the ever-moving point of the present moment. In this timeless moment, words on a page can connect with Presence.

Nonetheless, I am conscious of having drawn a Me-shaped circle round the point of infinite extension we called Glyn.

---

1. See Chapter 6. Rudyard Kipling: The Palace.

Prelude

LETTER FROM AN AMNESIAC

An evocation of the journey undertaken by those who remembers where they have come from, and decide to do what it takes to return.

I had forgotten.
I have been long away, mixing with strangers,
riding in their rough-wheeled cars,
watching their children bruising like flesh
of creamy petals in mud and churnings.
Amnesia, their word for my condition:
restless, unlabelled, like a piece of luggage
on a station ramp. Bear or bomb?
Either way a seat for Problems.

I mingled, not to spend my time
staring at a wall of the walnut
in the skull, temple of the faculties,
faculty where degrees are getting harder to come by.
I came by a couple in the course of time,
but have misplaced them.

Almost memories stirred sometimes
in the still, ticking night, when a curl of smoke
caressed the curtains of the room without;
or were missed, like an osprey on the mountains
in booming rocks and distance and coarse wild grass.

Only when your shadow fell upon me did I remember.
When you demanded love, and I found my supply
too short, and liquid, flowing hither and thither
and stored in a leaky vessel. I gave as I could:
the flame burned and died in an instant, but I glimpsed
an archway in the caverns of the heart,
and beyond it, the skies of our land.

II

I was a long time building a vehicle sound
and indestructible for such a Journey,
learning to distil the fuel, thick and golden,
oil of many inward trees which ripened as sun
percolated through my fitful soil.
I graduated from amnesiac into a fever
of too many memories where none had been,
and worked on, engineer in a science
ancient, artful, and most circumspect.

Your shadow lay over all my works,
the air full of the tang of you
and smiling on its secret like a child.
You came as many. I loved, you left,
and came again as another, and all the while
the golden fuel grew thicker in the cells.

III

One day I went, with no one looking on.
So slight the space I used, things moved through me,
hardly disturbing their dust.
I encountered the vastness where great planets swim,
the red, the ringed, the broad swirling lord;
and such distance, that Time picked craft
like rusty nits from its somnolent frame
and breathed out a galaxy in its sleep.
Prepared I was for solitude and hazard,
bones behind and wraiths before,
but with them came a wind from a far-off sun,
the scent of cypress and morning in the land of my birth.

A dry machine, consuming the gods of antiquity,
but one by one their perturbations coalesced
and sped me through epi-systems of the heart
into the wider waters and ranges of the inner stars.
Gnat-wings, comet-tail, sun-body and soil-cycle
lattice the laws of mind without,
mind in which I swim, body in which my body
moves its dance of love and suffering.

I see you now, waiting on a hill, and have come home.
As one, we fling another gaudy banner
to the winds of time and circumstance
that forgetful ones may see it and remember.

Chapter 1

A Portrait

How do you recognise a Man or Woman of Knowledge, the kind of Knowledge which is distinct from learning, cleverness, good intentions, wise insight or forcefulness?

If I had an idea how such an individual might appear, it would not have survived the encounter with the subject of these reminiscences, who confounded any conventional expectations of the Great Teacher, but quietly laid a foundation for a re-formulation of authentic philosophy.

We nearly lost him at Summertown, Oxford, in the summer of 1976, when he stepped into the path of a car in the Banbury Road, and was just yanked back in time. Saved by a whisker! He was unfazed, but it stuck in my mind as an uncharacteristic lapse of attention in a man whose life work revolved around Observation, Investigation and Experience, which he called the Three Modes of Attention. In this case, observation had slipped a little out of balance with the other two!

When Glyn and what we called 'The Work' entered my life it opened a whole new dimension. It was as if I'd been living in a small room with a balcony, only to discover that it was situated within a multi-roomed mansion with cellars, garden and private chapel, all open to me if I chose to investigate! Or indeed, like Plato's cave, I could turn away from shadows on the wall and face the authentic world beyond, if I held the intention to do so.

How does one recognise such authenticity, especially if it is not on a dais with flowers addressing a multitude?

I think of Glyn in any social context. What did he speak from? He needed no props, no badge, and you listened—a whole room would gravitate round this stocky little figure with the long-hair, nicotine stained fingers and cigarette burns on a grubby jumper (sometimes turned inside out for the benefit of the clean side). He could look more presentable in clean gear and jacket on public occasions, but the shoes usually had no laces, just holes—he had a 'thing' about laces.

Not everyone was enchanted, however. Some ran a mile, and he terrified others.

When you looked into his eyes you saw no-thing, no-one. Just a vast space...

His angle of vision was always unexpected, but always coherent, and when you examined it, opened up new ways of thinking. When I first met him in the early seventies, he was just embarking on his phase of gathering people to help with his self-generated task of re-formulating old philosophical ideas for modern understanding, in particular, the Kabbalah, which was the basis of his training. In the newly enlivened esoteric and spiritual context of London in the sixties, new ideas arriving from the East mingled with a re-discovered Western heritage. Magic, mysticism, meditation, astrology, esoteric lodges, spiritualism, theosophy were supplemented by elements from Jung and psycho-analysis, and the Gurdjieff/Ouspensky work presented a de-mystifying corrective to exotic and florid hocus-pocus. Glyn emerged from all this with a clear sense of a job to be done: to unclutter the fantasies and superstitions which accrete round any religious/esoteric way, and look to first principles in the roots of actual experience.

His bearded face was open, well-shaped, and his gaze steady and appraising. Around his eyes were crinkle lines. The eyes usually gleamed a little as he looked at you, and a rumbly laugh was never far away, shaking his form quietly at the absurdity of the human condition. '*Hours of innocent merriment*' was a stock phrase. He would, mischievously apply it sometimes to an apparently serious endeavour, either of his own, or some other exercise in which a great deal of pompous self-investment was evident.

His headquarters for nearly forty years was the Kitchen, tucked away at the back of a typical old west London apartment block. The Kitchen modified slightly over the years, but in general it presented mushroom–coloured walls with a huge brown and yellowing Tree of Life emblem on one wall, and another circular diagram painted on another. Glyn would preside from a large ancient chair, and all others would perch on a variety of old wooden chairs, some minus their backs, and one other semi-comfortable albeit elderly arm-chair. Ash-trays abounded, and in the early years, your eyes would sting with the smoke-haze as most people smoked continuously. A rickety window would sometimes be propped open with a pole, allowing a freezing draught to circulate round your feet, which turned into solid blocks by the end of the evening. Glyn rolled his own cigarettes from a round yellow tin of Boar's Head. In later years, concerned for his health perhaps, he inserted the wobbly fag into a holder, initially constructed himself from a ballpoint pen. Later he graduated to proper holders, but the elegant impression was always pleasingly incongruous.

In addition to aching buttocks and back, stinging eyes, and feet like ice, one's upper section got rather warm. My face used to flush like a tomato from the heat of the single gas burner on the grubby stove, which was the sole form of heating in the winter. I learned to wear thick boots if possible, and old clothes which could go straight into the wash, as the smoke penetrated right to vest and bra. This used to amaze me as I picked them up next morning, smelling as if I'd been barbecued the night before.

Glyn's entertainment came from devouring fiction, especially SF, and from an old television perched on a cupboard. He enjoyed watching what we tactfully called his "rubbish", and would often make you wait if you sprang on him unexpectedly, until some cop drama or the hapless geriatric escapades in 'Last of the Summer Wine' (a particular favourite) had finished. I never quite fathomed where his vast erudition came from, especially in pre-internet days. He kept up with documentaries of course, and had read very widely for many years, with a reading card at the British Library, which partly accounted for his extensive general knowledge and ability to discuss the most minute detail of just about anything with just about anyone. But it was the way he processed information which was unique. He incorporated it into some internal processor unlike anything I have ever encountered. He handled maths and scientific concepts with precision, and used them in the reams of delicate and detailed diagrams he generated constantly to back up, and indeed inspire, his metaphysical theorizing.

His background was in electrical engineering and accountancy, and he was an intensely practical man. He loved to make things, and to make things work. He called it 'boot-strapping' a term derived from his days in the air-force after the war. Boot-strapping, as I understand it, meant you picked yourself up by your own boot-straps, not relying on anyone else. (A gymnastic feat, but worth the effort!). For example, part of ritual training was making things from the most basic materials, not purchasing ready-made. To make a knife for ritual purposes, you boiled up the fish-oil to make the glue, cut and tempered the blade in a fire, twined a rope together, and used it to wrap into a handle. That kind of basic! The physical was an analogy for other levels of operation. '*Back to first principles*' was the most fundamental principle of every aspect of his teaching.

The Kitchen

The Kitchen was not a serious place. He liked to laugh, and in keeping with the 'no guru' rule, we all took the mickey whenever we could. It was an achievement to make him laugh, so we all tried, and he enjoyed witticisms. Puns were a special favourite, and he came up with some delectably awful ones himself. He was immensely patient though, when I look back on all the raw young talent he had to deal with, constantly. We would ring up and ask to come around then and there, somehow assuming he was always available for our benefit, or would always be pleased to discuss the solemn ideas of aspiring Knowledge-seekers. He almost never refused, and welcomed you with a quizzical look as you walked in the door, assessing where you were at. "What news?" he'd say, leaning back in his chair and puffing.

The conversations would go on into the small hours. It was common knowledge that the best stuff happened well after midnight, so we would wait it out, feeling the feet solidify and the cheeks start to burn. The conversation got deeper. If there had been an assorted crowd in the kitchen (you never quite knew who would be there, or from how far away), the less determined gradually peeled off and went home, leaving the hardy to push the conversation into more intimate areas of metaphysics or gossip. It was like being fed. You finally stumbled off into the silent streets, hoping your car hadn't been boxed in by double-parking, feeling replete and inwardly humming with a sort of psychic food, and possibly pages of scribbled notes. A visit to Glyn provided many weeks of internal stimulus.

His various personal peculiarities included not liking to have his hair cut (like Samson, I used to think) and it was most often tied into a pony-tail behind him. The absence of shoe-laces was owed to some very rational justification which I quite forget (he was heavy-footed when he stood and walked), and he went through a phase of wearing a bizarre house-dress like a jellaba made by his wife, instead of trousers. More comfortable, he asserted, and flicked the ash down his rotund middle, where little holes appeared, and a few assorted stains.

Once he startled us all by briefly shaving off his beard. It was not popular as his chin was unexpectedly small. Normally he had the face of a traditional prophet or guru: an ample greying beard and moustache, well-proportioned nose, and eyes which saw right into your soul and the soul of the universe. It was a noble head. He looked the part.

You could get lost in the eyes though. Later in his life I used to deliberately stare into them, trying to see how far I could go, or if I could find anything. Because later in life he lived more and more on what has been called 'Planet Glyn'. It was harder to connect with him. His voice sometimes trailed off as if he realised people weren't following, and indeed I often was not.

He also wept. Tears would just emerge as he talked, especially at the mention of anything carrying a certain type of emotion—you could call it higher emotion, which wasn't personal and involved humanity at its best: tales of people doing kindnesses, the ritual of royalty, the ethos of the Commonwealth, accounts of death or birth. He would wipe his eyes and carry on talking.

His presence carried such charge, that once, leaving, I got as far as the front steps before the whole fabric of my being seemed to disintegrate into a huge void. What was left stood pressed against the door, the rest blown away; everything I thought was me, gone. What I'd come to talk about was completely obliterated. How did that happen, I thought? We just chatted.

He never ceased producing material, right up to his final brief illness, methodically sketching neat little diagrams, transposing figures, weighing up propositions and terminology and generating new angles and theory to re-formulate the laws of the Eternal. It was always unexpected. He could turn things on their heads, and would try out new ideas on everyone who came through the door. We were his sounding-boards. He liked to be challenged and to engage in a good argument, testing out what worked and what didn't. His regular revisions of theory kept us all busy for nigh on 30 years, exploring and developing what he expounded as the latest way of looking, religiously copying the latest diagram to take back to whatever groups we were in. 'Glyn's new diagram' was a prize to be shared.

In later years fewer people came, but he never stopped generating, late into the night when all was quiet, and throughout the day as well.

He was always interested in other people's productions too, and was pleased when someone had done some original work. He regularly threw out tit-bits of ideas and stimuli, hoping they would be picked up and developed. Often, they were too 'far-out' for the recipient to be able to relate to, and fell on fallow ground. In the early years when we were running a centre, he was an active, almost explosive presence, directing, steering, pulling extraordinary rabbits out of hats, and generally creating an atmosphere of sheer magic and high adventure. The world was always richer around Glyn; the curtain of the mundane world pulled back to reveal wonders; the spirit bowed down to earth and was just about graspable.

He was never unkind; irritable sometimes, ruthless when need be; humble, he kept nothing for himself, owned practically nothing and refused all charity, even if possible, from the state. Until pensionable age he mostly worked, but had very little money. After a heart scare in middle age, he refused the recommended pace-maker, declining to have a mechanical object in such a symbolic role. Responsibility for your own actions was a rule he taught and lived by. He could be fierce, and dealt harshly with some of the men on occasion. There was always a little frisson of trepidation when going to see him, as cherished notions might get knocked for six, but I remember going to see him once expecting a rap over the knuckles for something and met only kindness and gentleness. I came away with my heart rejoicing, and feeling unexpectedly stronger. Visits almost always tuned you in to something greater and reminded, one way or another, but you could never be sure which way.

He trained us thoroughly in all the traditional esoteric skills and practices, if only so there would be no veil of mystique. '*We are generalists*' he would say. Specialized in no particular area, a generalist has a little experience of all, enough to know the basic principles and be able to design or re-create should the knowledge be lost. It gives a very clear-eyed and sober appreciation of how the psyche works to generate human life and interaction, and is excellent insurance against glamour and inflation. *'As necessary' is the golden rule. Speak and act only as necessary.*

Authority

He had a personal rule of which he regularly reminded all who came:—he would not keep secrets. Everything was passed on. It was a way of preventing the confidences of the self-important (which we all were) from accumulating round him, and then being used to manipulate him or others. (eg. asserting authority: "I went to see Glyn and he…") It was not possible to manipulate Glyn. He kept nothing for himself and owned nothing, material or other.

I frequently had the experience of hearing something I had told to him repeated back to me by someone else, particularly if it reflected badly on me, and someone was trying to set me straight! Galling, but effective. So much human interaction consists of power-games, trying to steal a march on another, present oneself as important, thoughtful, clever; to imply that one has the approval of an authority figure. But Glyn wouldn't play.

'Authority is given, not taken. People give authority to others, be it wise or unwise', was his stand on the cause of so much grief and violence as it plays out in the world.

By repeating to everyone who passed through his kitchen whatever was current, he prevented any log-jams of personal authority. It was not for the sake of gossip, though he liked to know what was going on, but any personal stuff was fair game for sharing. Deeper matters, such as from meditation checks or more profound conversations, was safe from this however. You instinctively learned to tell the difference. If it would not have mattered if it had been passed on, it wouldn't be, simply because it was not personal, not a secret and there was no power-seeking involved.

This practice was one of his deadly tricks to puncture self-importance, which is the greatest obstacle on a path of Knowledge. The greatest challenge for a teacher is the task of helping others to get beyond their natural egotism in a way which doesn't diminish them, but encourages growth and development of Being. It's one thing to give out teachings, but creating conditions to provide the shocks and provocations for change and self-insight is quite another.

So, despite his protestations not to give him authority, naturally everyone did, and sought his approval and imprimatur stamp for their ideas, theories and projects. One of two things would happen. Either the Great Project evaporated before your eyes once you'd aired it in his presence, and for no very clear reason, because there'd been no criticism. Or he chattily explored it with you, using it as a jumping off point for whatever was pre-occupying him at that time. You went away pleased, and somehow convinced of his approval. Except he hadn't actually given it. He'd just encouraged you to do more of what you were determined to do anyway.

Rather than trying to change people or their ideas, he maintained it was often better and more useful to re-enforce them, so that if there were cracks or weaknesses, they would become apparent to the person him or herself sooner rather than later. If there is a crack, widen it. If a weakness, drive a wedge in. He employed this strategy consistently, and articulated it frequently as a useful methodology. *'Make the inevitable happen'.* Hence, people would make their own assumptions along the lines they desired, and would depart with a comfortable assurance of authority bestowed.

However, because: a) you had accorded the authority yourself, and b) there were no secrets, quite often your plans would later sneak up and hit you in the back from another quarter, because he would have told everybody, and probably not in the flattering terms you might have wished for. Others would gain a different impression of whether or not he approved!

In all this Glyn was absolutely upfront. He told everyone his strategies as a teaching point, but it was hard to believe him when it came to oneself. They were simple principles, consciously employed, and he would sigh and shake his head theatrically when he was accused of 'manipulating'. He faced these accusations often, because it is human nature to invest authority in others, and then blame them if your expectations are not met.

I think Glyn made such an issue of authority, and of his own non-Guru role, because there is no issue more important in the individualist and turbulent Age we live in than understanding the nature of authority. The question: *To whom or to what are you giving authority?* underlies every conflict situation, every ideology. It is the nub of morality, aggression, victimisation, and all 'beliefs'. Secular Humanist philosophies give ultimate authority to ourselves as Humans. Others bestow ultimate authority on something outside us: Spirit, Consciousness, God. And finally, when artificial intelligence mimics human intelligence, will we give or withhold authority to the algorithms which apparently know us better than we know ourselves, and what would that mean in practice?

These are not academic issues, but day to day realities. Just about all human interactions are shaped by authority and the power which goes with it. The principle that authority is given not taken is transformative and fundamental, and Glyn lived it out with every person he encountered.

Self-responsibility means standing on your own feet. Otherwise "*Where will you be when your One has passed away?*"[1]

His methods were based on a view that the essence of Knowledge is common to all humanity, and on equality and self-responsibility, but did not pander to natural egotism, or ambition, or the wish to be given the fruits of wisdom and peace without effort. He set up situations in the early years when he was still actively engaged in training, but it was for purposes of the Work, not to play with people.

He could travel into the future with an enormous vision of humankind in the Multiverse. And into the past, with an impressive knowledge of history and a unique way of seeing relationships and the forces governing events. Forty years ago, when Islam seemed a benign, quiet presence on the world stage, I remember him warning that the big trouble to come was going to arise from Islam. It surprised me, as at that time many of us had links and great sympathy with Sufi groups and saw Islam mainly in terms of profound Sufi mysticism. I think of his prophecy every time a new Islamicist atrocity hits the headlines.

One day he announced he was learning Basque, a language with a unique root among languages and confined to a particular small area in the world, and where he intimated there could be an old tradition of knowledge. He found and hired a tutor and studied his dictionary diligently. With its help he then translated and presented in Basque some contemporary formulations of ancient principles.[2] That it would require considerable effort to access them, reflects their value, and 'burying the bone deeper' is designed to activate the teachings, not conceal them. It's especially salient in an age when everything appears accessible and just there for the taking. Growth through consciousness is never like that.

He lived longer than he expected, having withdrawn from active steering in most capacities long before, and offering only 'technical advice' for many years. He had a little pottery Urn made all ready for his ashes, and everyone passed it daily as it sat on a shelf in the dim hallway. He seemed to have been preparing for a long time, and was entirely ready to take a journey into the realm of 'the Player on the other side' as he liked to refer to the Divine mystery. You felt he loved that Player. He would talk God in any one's language, quoting from mystics, Christian, Kabbalist, Buddhist or any other tradition, emphasizing that the God we know is '*God in you*'. Some conversations about the spiritual I had with him seemed to leave the earth; I only took away fragments jotted down afterwards, but the impression of an immensity opening up was awesome.

It wasn't even in the words; it was something about the space created in his presence, and love was in the space.

---

1. The Book of Jubilee, Cranswick Press 1984
2. http://www.sareoso.org/

Chapter 2

Background

Of the three elements weaving through my recollections, Glyn, esoteric work, and my own personal story, this section focuses mainly on the collective and communal aspect, giving an impressionistic and personal overview of many years' common involvement.

I encountered the Work when I had been living in Oxford for a couple of years, working at a Bookshop in the Broad, and returning each evening to a tiny room down the Iffley Road. I had arrived from Australia at the age of twenty-two with no very clear intent as to future plans, and spent my first summer in Cambridge where I had friends. When I looked for somewhere to settle, Oxford seemed the natural choice, not too far from my sister in London and another sister in Wiltshire, though at that stage I had no further study in mind.

My rather bizarre little room was graced with an avocado-coloured bed, orange-striped carpet and purple curtains, but it also had a French window opening onto a garden with a gnarled old crab-apple tree like a large bonsai. I covered the ugliness of the spindly formica table with a thick creamy cloth bought as a remnant, and placed it in front of the window with a bowl of orange fruit. Faced with this painterly tableau, I could ignore the lurid hues of the rest of the room.

One afternoon, in the dying stages of a love affair I had expected to determine the course of my future, and therefore in a somewhat bruised and fragile state, I went to a party and began the chain of encounters which really did determine the course of my future. Although we didn't manage to speak, I noticed a man of rather singular appearance who looked at me piercingly across the room. As I was leaving, he pressed his details into my hand, saying: 'Ring me.' It was almost a command; the man had an unusual presence. So, when I was at a very low ebb some weeks later, I remembered the card he had given me, and decided I had nothing to lose by following it up.

The day I rang that mysterious number, everything changed, and the esoteric entered my hitherto conventional world. Although our acquaintance was brief, this man acted as a sort of usher and opened up a different reality to me. He personally inhabited a psychic-tinged world where meaningful and paranormal things happened, events had significance and strange powers were possible. It was he who first introduced me to the persons and teaching which became so central to my life.

At my phone-call, he immediately dropped everything he was doing and forthwith whisked me off to a nearby Neolithic stone circle. In the late afternoon sunshine, we wandered among the stones, the first time I had visited a sacred site like this, and it was as if four thousand years of sacred history sank into my soul like an initiation. "Count the stones", he said, and I tried, unaware of the legend which says they cannot be counted—the tally always comes out different. Here was the King Stone standing alone in a field, there the King's men and the Whispering Knights. Indeed, there seemed much whispering in the mild air of that summer evening, but I was a neophyte, unused to interpreting the murmurs of the earth. I simply wandered and wondered.

However, my ontogenesis was beginning. Until then, a liberal arts education had given me the basics of civilized values, learning and skills, but now the page had turned, and from this point on a series of encounters, new ideas and horizons made everything I'd read and loved so far seem like scratching the surface of phenomena. I began to discern the underpinnings—realizing there are identifiable *laws* of manifestation which can be studied and observed, and discovering philosophy and metaphysics which made sense of experience and the 'whys' and 'wherefores' of existence. The undefined kind of Faith which had sustained me from a child began to be shaped by experience. Gradually I learned that attention is a power, and developing it along certain lines is transformative, making the mute universe come alive with a numinous light and profound generative darkness.

First Group

It all took time of course. The first big change was in my circumstances. Encouraged by my new contact, I found myself involved with post-graduate work in Ethnology and living in the leafy streets of North Oxford in a Lady Margaret Hall flat. But side by side with academic study, I began to explore esoteric threads which had bearing on the same mythological areas of interest, and began hosting a Kabbalah study group in my flat. In its contemporary form of a three-pillared glyph of the Tree of Life, the ancient teaching of the Kabbalah can speak to a modern sensibility and offers an ordering foundation for ideas and experience to put some structure on the inner world of the psyche and universe.

Two guides regularly came up from London to take the group, one of whom was Glyn. He loomed in my basement room, a jovial, challenging presence, manifesting huge interest in everything. He often came up early and we spent the day walking in the Parks or Port Meadow, and I took him to Dinner in Hall. Being young and dumb, I can't remember the subjects of those discussions, but my world gradually expanded, and the group flourished for several years even after I had left Oxford.

The basic Kabbalistic structure is three pillars in balance, and ten principles which act as lenses through which you can view the interconnections of events. On an analogy with erecting a building, or indeed of the body itself, once structural principles are in place, growth and expansion is possible. The psyche is no different. It helps to have a sense of its workings, not broad scale theories, but simple root principles handed down for literally millennia. The basic form of this model the two side pillars of the Tree represent the polarity of Force (active) and Form (passive), and the central pillar is named Consciousness, a mediating principle of awareness which is the third element in every situation.

This description of the Kabbalistic Tree reflects a modern interpretation of a very old tradition of Jewish mysticism, which surfaced in the West in the 12th century, and later became identified with several esoteric lines including Christian, contributing to history of the western oral tradition. Glyn was instrumental in a contemporary formulation, creating what is called the Extended Tree, a diagrammatic representation of four inter-leaved Trees symbolising the four levels or worlds of creation. This re-formulation, and the further work in the years which followed, was a mission developed from his own training and initiation, and also reflected the development of psychoanalysis, especially Jungian. It was a deliberate departure from the magical and occult associations with which the Kabbalah had become identified, and led to a psychological interpretation and standardisation of the model which became popular and influential through the work of others. We also worked with this standard model at that time, because its simplicity and complexity allowed for fruitful life-study and group work, even without a regular teacher.

Over the course of his long life, faithful to his stated aim of reformulating the Kabbalistic teachings in a manner neither magical nor traditional Jewish, only the roots of the original system are visible in the metaphysical system Glyn generated, but that is the nature of evolving wisdom.

Meditation and esoteric roots

One day early on when he was up in Oxford, Glyn suggested I should learn to meditate. "Oh, no", I said. "I'm calm enough already", imagining, perhaps, that meditation might turn me into some ethereal being, and I wanted to engage with gritty existence. But he insisted that it would be a good thing, and so we set up two chairs and he initiated me into the technique. I worked hard to follow the instructions, only slightly put off by the sound of light snoring from the other chair. He called a halt after half an hour, and carefully checked my experience. In the years that followed, any solemn pretensions I might have affected as I initiated others, were always punctured whenever I remembered that during my Great Initiation into the mysteries of meditation, Glyn had apparently fallen asleep. But he'd also said with a wry chuckle when later on I was trying to make sense of some meditational experience or other: "It's a voyage of adventure you're on, my girl!"

Right as always; and never the voyage you expect.

When he launched a weekly Friday night group in his London flat, I used to come down from Oxford every Friday and return on the last train. In this group we used a mythological model of cities and temples, each level introducing a deeper/finer aspect of inner experience. We learned how this kind of experience is generated and the links with body and breath by trying it out. The remnants of the Hippie era of drugs and flower-power still lingered, but we didn't need drugs or wafting incense. Wafting was not where Glyn was at; he had arisen from a traditional esoteric background and tough training which he never revealed in detail.

The snippets we knew included a locker-door in Germany where he had first seen a diagram of the Tree of Life when he was in the air-force in the early Fifties, and a teacher revealingly named John Smith somewhere in Hull, whom he used to visit, but was now dead. From his initiation and study of Kabbalah, his teacher sent him to learn from esoteric and occult schools available at that time in London. The ancient teachings of the East were newly breaking onto the Western scene and combining with powerful western currents including the magical. Some of these schools are still extant, but many have waned as eastern religions established their teachings firmly in the West, and esoteric and occult strains were tarnished by foolishness and fantasy.

The Greco-Armenian philosopher Gurdjieff was a strong and solid influence, his genuinely inspired wisdom teaching fitting the mythos of the times, employing a functional terminology and context geared to modern western life. It was easy to adopt terms like 'The Work', and utilise some basic 'Fourth Way' theory and concepts because of the timely resonance with Glyn's ethos and approach, but both the origin and subsequent development of the work Glyn instituted were independent and not related to Gurdjieff. Glyn was also strongly influenced by personal links with a Samatha meditation tradition,[1] and he later incorporated and expanded the Buddhist doctrine of Dependant Origination into his metaphysic. It was also a time when different types of meditation were establishing themselves in the West.

Glyn was a product of a transitional time, an era of group-work breaking new ground. But even more important, he was a product of something else. Engraved on my mind is an image of a man on a winter's evening, walking down that little street beside Charing Cross station in the heart of London, who suddenly saw, between one step and the next, a whole different world. He saw his own Nothingness and began to laugh out loud. With that perception of nothingness, he was free. And in this way, so he described to me many years later, his life changed. As a free being he spent the rest of his days trying to help others escape from their bindings.

I attended the London group as an Intellectual who never *saw* anything, whereas others in the group enjoyed exciting imagistic journeys and deeply symbolic encounters. Until the day when I added my feeble contribution to the descriptions of golden eagles and other splendid winged beings in the collective feedback:

"I just saw a few feathers" I said sadly.

Glyn snapped to attention. "What kind of feathers?"

"You know, those little spread-out feathers at the wing-tips."

And as I described them, I realised the point he was making. I had actually *seen* those feathers. They were clear then, as they still are now, and carried significance. Splendiferous imagery wasn't the point, or necessary. The *seeing* was important. Realising I could *see* was a break-through, and I explored the symbolic realm of cities and temples over the next couple of years with new fascination and confidence that I could engage with symbolism in an active and fruitful way.

In this non-verbal realm which condenses meaning and speaks directly to the psyche through a mythological framework, a City is a level of organisation (by analogy, in the psyche), and the Temple is the sacred impulse at its heart. Each level of city we explored had its own characteristics, which emerged as the group investigated and contributed their individual feedback. Depending on how well you tuned in, the characteristics tended to be common. For instance, one level of city was glass-like, crystal, and appeared to have no occupants. "We are too slow", Glyn explained. Time is faster at this level and creates the impression of crystal, as evidenced by crystalline imagery in mythology all over the world. Systematic explorations like these can organize the content of non-ordinary perception and experience so that they can be shared, interpreted and knowledge passed on.

Symbolic studies

My journeys to Paddington as I returned to Oxford after the group on Fridays were often facilitated by an intense young man in a tiny red Fiat car. This elderly little Fiat occasionally needed to be struck with a hammer to get it going, and I was a tall flowing creature in those days, with long hair and draping attire. It was apparently a comical picture as I emerged grandly from the small beat-up insect of a car, as he and I became an Item. We are still married to this day.

I had gained a Diploma in Ethnology, and went on to define a thesis topic for a D.Phil. This was naturally along the lines of my overwhelming interest in symbolism and the sacred, and had a title addressing the 'nature of Sacred Symbolism'. I had been encouraged by a friend native to the tradition to tackle the then little known and struggling-to-survive religion of Zoroastrianism. Diminishing in numbers through persecution and natural causes at its origins in Iran and India, the sacred texts, some of them dating from more than a thousand years BC, existed at that time mainly in dreadful translations by nineteenth century scholars. The old Avestan language, contemporary with Sanskrit, had not survived as well as the latter. Scholars had enjoyed a field-day with clunky interpretations of cow-based symbolism, stiff and lifeless depictions of deity-type figures derived from the available fragments of text and tradition, and dogmatic assertions about dualism and the doctrine of good and evil.

"There's got to be a better way to deal with a symbolic tradition and literature than this," I thought, and plunged into the dual task of researching Zoroastrianism and theories of symbolism. A major difficulty to my researches was lack of appropriate supervision. At that time there was no one suitable to guide me on the arcane and vexatious subject I had determined upon, one of my supervisors being an expert in outrigger canoes and the other a Christian monk. Undaunted, I decided that the best way to understand this sort of symbolic stuff would be to work with it, and get some practical understanding of how the mind creates symbolic forms and what sort of experience it is thereby clothing, particularly with religious imagery and mythology. The group-work I was already pursuing did exactly that, so in my mind, exploring esoteric symbols was also field-work. The only problem was that the academic got left far behind, and began to seem pointless, though I devoted three years to the research, hoping it might wind back to somewhere I could pick up again. But three years isn't enough for this sort of field-work, and it hasn't yet re-surfaced as an academic project.

When time ran out, I moved to London, not far from Glyn's habitation which he shared with his wife and two children. Other groups in the north of England had been running simultaneously with the Oxford group, and we all began to form a community. Glyn's constant re-formulation gave us plenty to work with, theory to try and flesh out, diagrams to study and decide what they meant in real psychological and metaphysical terms. '*Diagrams*', he said, '*speak directly to a higher level of creativity than the usual mind*'.

Because he was so unremittingly creative, waves of theory succeeded each other, some getting left behind as we moved on to the next, but all capable of being picked up and used as the basis of an approach to inner work. I earnestly copied diagrams from whiteboards, or from pieces of paper or his large old diaries which Glyn would thrust at us in his kitchen. As I copied, I was sure that one day I'd understand much better, because other people seemed to have a much more focussed grasp, especially of the mathematics and geometry underlying the created forms amongst which we live.

At the simplest level of symbolism, it all comes down to number. Those who were more naturally mathematically minded worked with him to refine and elaborate details over the years. I struggled a bit with the numbers, but accepted that this was also training, extending my natural bent into new areas, and cultivating *abstract mind.* I was more at home with narrative and explanations, and the active group discussions arguing about the meaning of these formulations. Glyn's mind would work from number, the abstract, outwards into new ways of perceiving and understanding experience. It was his creativity and genius to do this original work.

Questioning everything, translating it into experience was foundational to our way of working. Glyn reiterated: '*Questions are more valuable than answers. If you can compose the right question, you can find the answer'.*

Again and again he would say: *'Answers close doors. Questions open them.'* So, we let nothing pass without lots of heated analysis and discussion under certain rules of group discipline, which at the same time performed the function of knocking corners off our personal self-importance. There was method in this. In normal social interactions, largely to avoid a free-for-all of passionate opinions, group discussions are usually either constrained by politeness, or limited by lack of a common vocabulary, which necessitates careful diplomacy and a lot of time to unpick each person's individualistic meaning-frame. The advantage of working with a disciplined framework and established common understanding of terms, is that questioning can be direct, penetrative and lively. I will say more about this process in Chapter 5.

'*If you don't ask the question, you won't get the answer*' is something I had to learn. The gold of Knowledge needs to be actively sought and won. Waiting for it to descend, or personal diffidence and self-consciousness may not yield this treasure, hence it is written: "the kingdom of heaven is taken by storm".

Saros

From 1978, guided by Glyn, we had formed ourselves into an organisation with a public name and identity. The name Saros, appropriately, came from sticking a pin in a dictionary. Equally appropriately, it is a Babylonian word referring to an alignment of sun, moon and earth every 18.33 years. It was perfect symbolism for our purposes: sun, moon and earth can stand for the head and intellectual function, the heart and emotional being, and the body and action—the three broad centres of the human organism.

Knowledge arises from a creative balance between these three areas. If the head or conceptual ability becomes very dominant, as it can be in some intellectuals, it may be at the cost of emotional maturity, and/or the physical body which is given little attention. Some intellectuals hardly seem to inhabit their bodies. On the other hand, emotional people tend rely on their feelings for everything and could not structure a well-reasoned argument to save their lives, and the body may be abused in various ways. Then there are physical or sports-oriented individuals who may live in a world of muscle and sweat, with little interest in abstract thought or emotional nuances. These are extremes, but not uncommon, and all combinations and degrees make up the natural range of humanity.

We're all born with different capacities and predilections, but concentrating solely on our natural talents or skills does not further well-rounded development. If we also work on the areas we find hardest or are weakest for us personally, not only do we extend our abilities, but it develops awareness of others, patience, humility and maybe some wisdom. The purpose of an esoteric education, as compared with paths which specialise in one or another aspect (I can think of heart-based, body-based or highly intellectual paths—all perfectly valid) is to *balance* the organism and its centres of energy and function.

So as part of our education, Glyn would suggest we undertake varied training. We defined Saros as an educational organisation. People maintained active links and allegiances to other 'paths', some religious, some involving movement or martial arts. Any expertise involving skill and attention can be useful for the development of consciousness, particularly if it is outside your own natural range. I practised Bagua and Kung Fu at one stage, and oriental dance. Others learned tango, archery, icon painting, sword and staff fighting, stained glass and many other crafts with a traditional background. We were encouraged to read and study other traditions, and to visit a range of groups.

As Saros, we established a Centre in the Peak District of Derbyshire for holding long courses and weekends, and for renting out to other sympathetic organizations. Intense work and a lot of laughter filled these years. Although courses had taken place before the establishment of our Centre, it made things easier. The traditional smoky atmosphere prevailed in the Long Room, and many sofas and arm-chairs lent themselves to late-night discussions, presided over by Glyn if he was there. Another large clear room served as the work-room, either lined with trestle tables, or cleared for movement, dance or ritual. The third communal room was the meditation room, a silent space which the evening sun would grace as it sank over the moors.

We decorated and painted the centre ourselves on Work Weekends, which were an ideal combination of inner discipline with outer practical activity. Somehow the woodwork of the upper corridor with the bedrooms leading off, turned out a bright fiery red. Someone got the colour chart a bit wrong here, and going to bed was a journey into the landscape of hell.

After about seven years, collectively through an AGM of members, it was decided to let the Centre go. It had served its purpose, and the burden of maintenance had fallen disproportionally on people in the north of England. It was more than a four-hour journey from London, but none the less, Londoners did it very regularly, and others from the West endured more than five hours of travel each time. Petrol was cheaper then, and it seemed normal to go back and forth, winding through the stone walls, valleys and hills of the Peak District once we left the motorway. My usual frame of mind included an element of dread mixed with anticipation, as I wondered what challenges might lie ahead. One's comfort zone was not an item on the agenda of any Saros gathering. As a butterfly emerges from a pupa or a cicada from its shell, being comfortable contains no stimulus for growth and can become an imprisoning cage. However, breaking out may take quite a while; and then there's the wait for the wings to dry!

Saros as an organization was a training ground on many levels, administrative, political and inter-relational as well as providing a stage for people to develop their individual talents and skills. Bi-annual public Saros Seminars were held in London with a range of well-known, not in-house speakers. The seminars were intended to spark debate and challenge the conformity of fashionable views on contemporary issues, not to present a particular view. Education, death, the future, religion, morality were some of the topics covered. The task of organizing these events was part of the training.

In later years Glyn said that he had seen a large part of

his function as keeping us 'entertained'. Many projects and activities were not necessarily important for their own sakes, (as we thought at the time) but because they allowed for constructive engagement, learning through doing, not just thinking, and through collaboration over time. Activities, projects, ideas for people to follow up were Glyn's solution to restlessness, impatience or ambition. It served the simple purpose of keeping us busy while the processes of maturation took their course, as they will, given enough time and direction. But keeping people, or oneself, travelling in the same direction when the natural tendency is to expect results and switch to something else if they don't eventuate, is a tall order. Over and over again Glyn would insist: '*Don't look for results. You work for the Work's sake; meditate for the sake of meditation. Don't look for personal gain.*'

However, it demonstrates that it is possible to follow a path of Knowledge in the world, in the midst of everyday conditions. It's very hard to keep working without personal benefit unless the aim is clear, and unless kept busy. At one point I had two small children, was writing a book, running two groups and attending a couple of others. Sometimes it seemed too much and I nearly cracked. Once when it all got on top of me, I remember hurling down a spoon while trying to feed the children and running out into the street, resolved never to return. The problem was my bare feet. I got as far as a bench a little way up the hill, and there I sat and reflected upon how far I could get with no shoes on the filthy London pavements, and no money either. Presently I slipped back into the domestic scene where my husband had calmly taken over my role, and I resumed the supper routine.

Work for the Work

We took ourselves seriously, and the Work seriously which, in a way, is necessary in order to hold focus and intention amid the many distractions and concerns of living. But it is good to be reminded of the Cosmic Laugh, the perspective which is elsewhere called 'Maya', just in case we take ourselves and our importance too seriously.

I heard the Cosmic Laugh once, in a high energy situation. The course, not run by Glyn himself, had been charged, full of magic and wonder, until I stepped into an empty room one night on my way to bed. It had been the work-space during the day, and the atmosphere was still vibrant, humming with a fine energy. Then it all collapsed. Just like that. The whole fabric turned to ash and I stood, a lonely figure, on the edge of an abyss of nothingness. Then I heard laughter, Glyn's it seemed, vanishing like a spiral into the upper right corner of the room. The joke? I'd been 'had'. I knew it then, that everything—the course, the years of work, life itself—is a creation, and that creation had just dissolved for me. I hear the laugh still.

Fortunately, as it does, dawn brought a new creation. I passed a bad night in the void, and in the morning opened the curtains. For a split second nothing was there, then the world literally re-constructed itself before my eyes, and fields of sheep, trees and mountains appeared. A little slower than usual, they came together under the power of the Creator, and how beautiful they were, those sheep which safely grazed!

In hindsight, I missed something at the time. I never asked the question: Who remained? Who stood on the edge of the void, who lay weeping for all that was gone, and who witnessed the resurrection of the world? It took many more years before I turned my gaze from what was gone, to what remained. We insist on engaging with a created fabric, the veil of Maya, and it is our curse to expect to benefit our fat selves from this gauzy light-show!

As the years passed, the 'no personal gain' rubric bit deeper. Perhaps it actually meant exactly that? Who does anything for no gain? Under Glyn's masterly direction, we did, though we didn't really believe the 'no gain' bit at the time. And time passed. And as time passed, we grew older, raised children, studied diagrams, put on shows, learned movements, read books and matured in understanding. There were costs, of course, personal costs. Another of Glyn's repeated phrases was: '*No such thing as a free lunch*'. There are things I regret, that I might have done differently; some are important things, but I kept faith with the Work as I saw it. No such thing as a free lunch.

To train the body, movements were designed to be performed slowly, with absolute attention, and called the Balance Dance. It involved maintaining balance on one leg while slowly moving the arm and head in different ways, and contending with gusts of wind and the irritation of struggling to keep up, getting it wrong and falling over. But after long sessions of this outside, Nature seemed to co-operate, and silence grew intense. Was that silence outside, or inside? Hard to tell.

We elaborated the meditative art of Turning (along the lines of Mevlevi whirling dervishes) into a public performance with a whirling banner and swords, spinning in various formations to the rhythmic flap of the banner, with a quiet chant ebbing and flowing. If you can get over the fear which leads to dizziness, there is grandeur in the combination of stillness and movement, even for spectators. It involves holding one's body axis absolutely steady, as in meditation, while the world turns around. One foot stays flat while the other propels in a circular motion. In the centre of all that motion is an immense stillness, and joy.

There was a more 'esoteric' side, in the hidden sense, which was different from the work groups, seminars and study groups which were open to anyone. In the invitation-only groups we worked with a specific mythology designed to operate with the inner senses and train the use of energies. It also helped us understand the psycho-logic of ritual action, and how to bring a mythological, metaphorical framework to life, and into life. I will say more about our ritual activities in chapter 8. Glyn presided over the formation of these groups and was available for advice on any technicalities, but never actually took part.

We were heirs to the era of flower-power and spontaneous research into mind-altering substances and their role in consciousness, but drugs weren't on the agenda— others had opened those doors. For our purposes, their value as indicators and initiators of non-ordinary potential was heavily outweighed by other negative factors. Besides which, we were mostly poor, and the exigencies of pursuing the Work took all the finances and time most of us had at our disposal. Worldly high-flyers we were not, in the main. A high-powered job would leave little time for esoteric pursuits, and common wisdom decrees that you have to make choices in life.

The Saros of Saros (astronomically 18.33 years) passed with various celebratory events, and in 2001 the organisation itself was dissolved by a collective EGM decision, and the few accumulated funds distributed among then members. No longer having a collective platform was, and is still, a real challenge for all those trained under its umbrella. But until his death Glyn continued to preside from his kitchen, organising his theoretical work for an internet age, and hiding his work in plain sight by rendering it into Basque. It is there for the determined to access!

1. The Samatha Trust http://www.samatha.org/

Chapter 3

Antecedents

A waltz through some aspects of my own background and story, looking to identify those elements which drew me to this sort of Work. The quest for true identity.

Until I made the phone call which launched a new phase, as a student and young person finding my way in life I had turned to art, literature and poetry, philosophy and religion in general. I was brought up in a staunch Catholic family, and I treasured this heritage and followed it faithfully right up until the time I quietly let it go as a young adult. Not rejected, not carelessly or casually misplaced; that rich and formative background laid many foundation stones which continue to prove their worth. But I needed to move into fresh fields.

My attitude perhaps contrasted with that of many of my youthful contemporaries in the late sixties and seventies who rejected the religions and values of their birth with vehemence. It was an era characterized by student protests (the Vietnam War particularly in Australia), the rise of Women's Lib, gay rights and youthful political activism. The Beat generation of the fifties and early sixties had shaken up all 'conformist' social values with intensity and anti-materialism, and in its origins, it was a determined visionary attitude, ('beat' from 'beatitude, beatific') which was unfairly caricatured by the media stereotype of the 'beat-nik'. From a sense of displacement, of being an 'Outsider', arose a yearning for inner freedom, and led through seminal figures like Kerouac, Ginsberg, Alan Watts into interest in east Asian religions, and particularly Buddhism because its detached intellectual flavour appealed more than the Christian or Jewish roots of many of the restless western seekers.

Everyone is influenced by the times in which they live, but this kind of social fervour was tangential to my own early upbringing, where I absorbed poetry rather than protest, solemnly intoning poems learnt by heart on solitary wanderings through the scrubby bush or the great fragrant rainforests of my native Australia, or through the dunes beside the wild sea, across which I supposed was the rest of the world of "faraway places with strange sounding names, calling and calling to me". Australia was at the bottom of the globe. I would gaze with yearning to the horizon where the great white liners passed, and beyond which lay all those exotic places. Except that they didn't. Beyond the horizon I saw, lay the frozen wastes of Antarctica and some penguins.

So, the first lesson in extending perception is never trust a horizon! As a child, in the freedom of the outdoor life, I wandered long distances, just returning in time for afternoon-tea, the Australian term for a mid-afternoon snack usually involving biscuits or cake. It was accepted that I had extraordinary powers of hearing, and never missed the rattle of the biscuit-tin no matter how far away I had been, (several miles were not uncommon). My roaming was filled with contemplative imaginings, and was a kind of innocent, inborn Faith: faith that there is meaning in life, that there is a mystery hidden beneath the surface of things which one day I would plumb. I had made a passionate resolution formally to myself at about age twenty: to become a plumber of the infinite, and I never doubted it would be possible. The plumbing just probably lay over the sea, with the rest of the world.

Later at university, I read voluminously, from prescribed classics to the long and absorbing must-reads of the era like 'The Alexandra Quartet' by Durrell, Tolkien's 'Lord of the Rings', Nikos Kazantzakis, science-fiction epics like 'Dune', all of which had that quality of transporting a youthful reader on the cusp of adulthood into an emotionally rich and mythic realm. I still have a memory of many happy hours lying in the grass of a college garden, listening to the bees humming among the flowers and the bells chiming the hours from the chapel steeple. Hours of sheer bliss, young, with friends, and with all the unrealised future lying ahead like a mist. To literature I added some books of philosophy and comparative religion, as it dawned upon me that there might be alternative ways of looking at the big meaningful questions of life's purpose.

I had a certain determination behind the lotus-eating days of young adulthood. It manifested in the times when I absented myself from the social collections of disparate individuals smoking and drinking in the shared kitchen, in favour of moonlit hours listening to Beethoven whose brooding face glowered at me from the wall, and studying the patterns the streetlights made of the leaves outside the window. What was I up to? I can't really say—it was as if something was hatching. Those solitary hours were rich, as if pulling together threads from the Unknown, but without any particular shape. I wasn't interested in the 'Who am I' question back then, and from later experience I suggest that this drive may be more of a compulsion in young men. I thought I knew who I was, but wasn't concerned about giving it a name or identity.

The question of identity very much defines the twenty-first century era of spiritual search and spiritual teaching, so I shall follow this thread. Every now and again from early childhood, something happened to my normal psychological functioning and a strange state broke through. They may sound a little mundane in the re-telling, and I didn't flag them up as great mystical experiences, but they were each memorable for their potency, like ushers to another realm. I believe this kind of thing is quite common, but easily ignored or forgotten as 'just one of those peculiar happenings', and the tide of everyday life quickly closes over the ephemeral footprint.

It was as if another 'me' took over, and it was a shock to my normal system. I described them to myself as "slipping sideways", or that the world around had turned sideways, or had completely disappeared, momentarily. It was often a consequence of some irreconcilable conflict, and I never forgot these incidents because I really learned something. I suppose in hindsight I would say I *knew* something: but it was knowledge of a different order from normal ratiocination or perception. These slippages not only contributed to my sense that there is more to life and being than the familiar world appearance, but also provided pragmatic evidence of an alternative way of operating, or state of being.

In my final degree year, I was living with two close friends in a flat above a corner shop just by the university. The entrance was open to all through the shop at the back, so it was, that one day I was painting and decorating my room dressed in a shapeless mini sack, with paint-splattered un-made-up face (it was the era of heavily lined black eyes like Cleopatra), and my normally sleek long hair randomly skewered on top, when a visitor suddenly appeared in the hallway. It was a professor friend, a charming Lothario undoubtedly with seduction in mind as he appeared without warning at the top of the stairs. I had no time even to glance in a mirror, let alone repair or tidy up the shambles of my appearance, and the surprise and dissonance with my usual presentation produced a frozen moment, a sort of gap in continuity. Into this gap, and produced by its power, I simply dropped my self-image. I stepped out of my normal self like a garment, leaving a space in which Someone smiled and led the visitor into the dingy kitchen, seated him in the corner by the window and began to make coffee.

It wasn't 'me', exactly. Something else had been precipitated into coming forth by the shock, by being caught so unprepared and with no masks in place. It felt like radiance, a quiet power, a beauty which I could feel gracing all my movements as I sorted kettle and cups by the dim and grubby sink. When I looked over at my visitor, his jaw had dropped open and his eyes were glued on me with a look of wonder. "You are so beautiful…" he breathed, and I smiled. That was all; just a smile in the silence, because I knew thanks were totally inappropriate, as if a compliment had been addressed to *me.* He may not have known the difference, but I knew that Beauty, like a presence, almost a Being, had briefly come to dwell in me but did not belong to me. All I could truthfully do was acknowledge his acknowledgement. I never forgot this experience and any time I received a similar compliment thereafter, I knew it wasn't actually for me or anything I could claim to own or to be. Not *me*; they are seeing *It.*

One day I left the country of my birth, bound for the great unknown across the seas.

"The summer wind was nudging at the sand
Of that last night, shifting grain by grain.
Laissez..laissez..je vais with the black sea
Muttering far out into gaping lands:
The unforeseeable future, peopled with vast imagining
And doomed to diminution
Through the sucking mouth of Time…
Pass the chartreuse, all gritty with salt,
In a bevy of friends, supped and supine on the beach.
I am leaving them, unquestioningly, unexplainable,
But moving with the pull of multiplicity
And the one-shot law of life.

Knotting every shared hour into one night,
When laughter grew ragged,
We left before the dawn."[1]

Oxford

The next phase of my education took place in Oxford, into which I had merged seamlessly even before taking up further studies. I treated all the college gardens as personal fiefdoms for my wanderings (no security issues in those days), and continued the tradition of settling into some secluded flowery space with an inspiring book or three.

Every now and again, the mundane world would slip sideways a little.

After a trip to the library, I settled myself one day with a pile of new books and a large peach in the Oxford Parks. I chose a spot well into the central green space. It was a very perfect peach, which I lifted with anticipation to sink my teeth into its velvety surface, when a dirty old homeless man shuffled up and begged for a few coins. A worm had entered paradise. The peach instantly lost its savour as I rustled around and dug out some coins, but then I looked up. His eyes were gazing at me, blue and piercing, and in them— in him— I saw Him, 'the Lord', Christ, Krishna, by whatever name, who looked at me and *saw* me. The world briefly stopped, frozen. Again, it was a gap in the flow of time.

When time started again and I collected my wits, the beggar was gone. But I was in the middle of a clear grassy area; no one was near, so how had he disappeared so fast? I leapt up, still in a confused state and ran over to the path which lay behind a line of bushes. It stretched the length of the Park, empty, except for the small figure of a gardener working in the distance.

I was unable to explain the incident, but it was significant, one of those moments which are stored in perfect clarity. I have seen those piercing blue eyes again, on different occasions both inner and outer, in the years which followed, always unexpectedly, always with a whiff of another time, another place, another reality. Eyes through which some 'Other' looks, not the one in whose face they are set. Who perceives this Other? The common thread is not out there in different people, but in the internal shift which allowed me to perceive it.

On another occasion I was in a pub in the Lake District late in the evening, watching in some dismay across a crowded room, as a young boy who certainly should not have been there, was plied with alcohol by his laughing family. It was all a joke until the lad suddenly went slightly berserk, leaping up on a chair and screaming with wild eyes. I sensed the frenzy was real, like a mini-possession, and in the crisis something palpable went out from me, a long strand which reached him all the way over the other side of the room, soothingly. Immediately his eyes found mine, and he slid quietly down the wall into his seat, never taking his eyes off mine.

I hardly registered the incident consciously at the time. It takes a while for ordinary consciousness to catch up after an odd experience like this. It was only later as we were preparing for bed in a shared room, that a friend mentioned the curiosity of the wild boy and how suddenly he had gone quiet. Only then I remembered my part in it and the cord-like strand which had left my middle and traversed the space between. "Remember...before the silver cord be loosed, or the golden bowl be broken...". (Ecclesiastes 12.6))

I absorbed many influences during those Oxford years. An intense relationship with an Artist widened my understanding of visual Art, and introduced me to the mystical poet Rilke among others. My quest for meaning took an intellectual turn as I devoured the writings of the Traditionalist School, Rene Guenon, Shuon, Coomaraswamy, and the evolutionary theory of Teilhard de Chardin. These writers, with their insistence that sacred symbolism is a language operating on several levels simultaneously, allowing the significance to be penetrated in differing degrees according to one's understanding of the experience it clothed, probably seeded my long-term preoccupation with what I see as the pivotal and much under-respected role of symbol and mythic narrative in our lives. As well as reading a lot, I continued practical research through the study-group work, and tried to draw it all together into a respectable thesis argument.

It was while punting down the Cherwell that another little out-of-the-ordinary slippage occurred. In a group of friends, we had moored by the edge of a college garden, and taken a short walk, but when we returned, the two paddles provided with the punt were missing. Two boys had apparently been seen nearby earlier, and we assumed they were the culprits. So that was that, was the general conclusion. The oars were lost.

No, they weren't, I thought, and stood up purposefully. "Wait here. I'll get them back".

I had absolutely no idea in my head as I stood up; I had not seen any boys, I had no plan, no thought. I just simply and clearly knew I would get the paddles because it was not right for the paddles to be missing. So, with what I can only describe as a burning focus-point leading a no-one, my body set off straight as a rocket through the garden, a gap in the fence and into the wide, open space of a public park. There were people all over the very extensive field, kids, picnickers, dogs and players kicking balls. Without pausing to examine the options I headed unswervingly across the space to two boys near a log in the distance, whereupon I reached out my hand and demanded our oars back with a few choice words about embarking on a life of crime. Completely discountenanced by this unexpected apparition and peremptory demand, they reached under the log and produced the paddles, which I commandeered with a parting shot about the evils of entering a private garden, as I turned on my heel.

This was actually a little rich, as we had moored in a Fellows garden where technically we should not have been either, but I did not break stride as I marched back and presented the oars to my friends. "Here. Let's go." Again, it was only later when the focussed state had abated by degrees, that I wondered 'what on earth had got into me' – literally got into me.

Or rather: what had got *out* of me. Normal Me, full of thoughts and self-preoccupations briefly took a holiday, and what was left could operate just fine. Spontaneous states are like forerunners, intimations, so there is an inbuilt tendency to forget immediately afterwards, probably protective of the status quo because they don't fit with normal psychological operation. However, if fleeting experiences like these are noted, recognised and tucked away in an inner treasury of similar experiences, they may accumulate into a stimulus for enquiry, giving a taste of a different mode of perception. Perception is a window, and self-selected, not an inventory of reality.

Likewise, mind-altering drugs are not a doorway to truth. In the right conditions they can be educative and break up the fixity of everyday perception, which is a practice with a long history in different cultures. However, spontaneous shifts and proper training can open the same doors in a manner less subject to personal inflation and the delusions stemming from believing the *content* of the experiences. Meditation and similar practices can also transcend the scope of 'normal' as I found out much later. Nonetheless, it's important to take note of spontaneous occurrences or they will vanish into the sleep of forgetfulness, and without elaborating or aggrandizing, to store them like seeds in the darkness. Unusual powers, such as clairvoyance, or the superhuman strength which could lift a car off a child in a crisis, may accompany genuine shifts. In my punting experience, though a trifling example, I *knew exactly* where the oars were without having observed or figured out anything.

These spontaneous introductions to a more powerful aspect of my own Being simply demonstrated to me that it existed. In fact, I could trace intimations back into childhood of a shadowy power, a kind of 'livingness' within, but only rarely did natural conditions facilitate its emergence and operation. I just trusted it would arise if needed, which I think is the substance of Faith.

My experience does not support the widespread materialist theory of consciousness as an emergent phenomenon, emerging as a product when a certain level of complexity is achieved. As a gardener I have noted that a splendid flower will not emerge from the minerals and nutriments of the soil without there being a seed in position first, which itself is embedded in a network of hidden and antecedent orders such as previous generations, gardeners, birds etc. (Only weeds seem to be an exception to this law and spontaneously generate, but my perception could be flawed.)

From the perspective of esoteric science, the inter-weaving and chain of causality is sometimes known as Karma. The ultimate mystery is the beginning: emergence from no-thing, from the Void. Both material and esoteric science start and stop at this most potent of all mysteries, forever resisting the explanatory powers of human reason as to the 'why' or 'how'. The seed of *mystery* is the most valuable seed of all, its hidden life driving both material science research and the esoteric quest to understand the laws of the visible and invisible universe.

Esotericism

The strange incursions of a different 'me', as in these minor examples, was not the 'self' I was familiar with, yet it was definitely me and not some weird inhabiting Entity. It felt essentially the same on each occasion, functioning according to circumstances. But fifty years later my life-experience has accumulated into a 'substance' through which it can be expressed, laid down by all the choices and experiences I have lived through. It comes back to the question which much spiritual teaching takes as a starting-point: Who am I?

Before I encountered the Work, and Glyn, I tended to treat life as a gauzy fabric, and simply tried to follow its billowing movements, while peering with interest at what looked like mysterious shapes beneath its folds. I assumed there was some order to it all, if I could only discern what it was. And then Glyn blew in and cut through the silk, so to speak. He announced that indeed the billows are not random. They have an ordering which starts with 1,3,2, and every interaction is a product of three forces. Furthermore, the processes of life can be numerically ordered into seven cosmoses which stand in precise relationship to each other. Add to this the notion that every complete process can be divided into eight stages, and just like the musical octave, there are two points in that process where extra energy needs to enter to maintain the same direction, so that if you can recognise these points, you can complete what you start without veering or abandoning it... and so on. (See Chapter 7 for more explanation)

It made sense to me that the totality of the universe conforms to certain Laws of operation, known and expressed in many different ways for millennia, (eg Dharma, the Indian term). *Metaphysics* is not an expression of intuitive poetic insights, but the identification of precise structuring principles, a 'science', the meaning of which is 'knowledge'. Meta-physics is a science which includes and unifies non-material aspects of life and consciousness with those of matter. The laws of metaphysics, as distinct from the laws of physics, encompass all levels of reality, seen and unseen, known and unknown.

Just as sub-atomic particles are tracked in a cloud chamber or particle detector but not actually seen, the universal laws are like tracks which need the presence of a conscious detector. I am reminded of the seeker in the Song of Songs, searching for her Beloved by following the footsteps made by his flock: "Go thy way by the footsteps of the flock…" (1,v8). The finest 'matter', the finest experience, may be located only indirectly by following its tracks. Particle physics and metaphysics converge.

The esoteric cosmos I entered after I encountered Glyn was structured, and could be taken further and deeper than the intuitive and feeling-based impulses I had followed before. It was a whole new birth, intellectually stimulating, emotionally enriching and physically engaging.

As well as the 'slipping' incidents, which I tucked away somewhere inside as unable to be categorised, I had one overwhelming aim which predisposed me towards the esoteric. It was conceived as a child and expressed quite succinctly in the small Catholic Catechism booklet which we children learned by heart in our first convent school classes, and which we would recite in childish sing-song voices which echo still when I use the words. It was in the form of question and answer, and the opening Question One was a delightfully uber-succinct summary of basic doctrine: "Who made the World? God made the world." Question two or three was, as I recall from this vast distance in time: "Q: Why did God make me? A: God made me to know Him, love Him and serve Him, and to be happy with Him forever in Heaven."

The 'happy forever in Heaven' bit didn't grab me, but the first bit did. It settled inside me as the perfect summary of what I wanted from life: 'to know Him, love Him and serve Him', *in that order*. The order was most important. My mind was often exercised by what seemed like the absurdity of trying to love what you don't know. I couldn't imagine how I could possibly love some Creator conceived in my own imagination, some figment which I was aware I could certainly create if I tried and probably get very attached to. It puzzled me that priests and preachers seemed to have no such trouble, and promulgated all kinds of versions of this Supreme Being in tones of boredom or frenzy. What the hell are they in love with, I thought? Do they *know* what they are talking about?

If some mystery lay behind the familiar words of the Gospels, I wanted to *know* who or what it was. I didn't actually doubt the existence of the mystery; I just needed to experience it so that love would arise as the natural consequence, which again I did not doubt, rather than as some confection of my own emotional outpouring.

This still seems to me entirely reasonable. Back then it was the reason I embraced the challenge of Glyn and his abstract bent with total ease and acceptance. As a path of Knowledge, I assumed it would lead me to know what composed the fabric of the Real, call it God or what you will, and it had presented itself clearly as the first step to take. Also, it had found me, by a remorseless series of stages which I hadn't engineered. I rather hoped it would fit with 'God', the word which is a universal shorthand for something primary, but the word 'God' itself troubled me. Even then I felt it had been so profaned, wielded in so many dubious and dangerous contexts, and given so many both dull and colourful attributions that it had become a liability, and I was quite happy to park it on one side until I knew more of what I was dealing with.

It still seems that invoking 'God' is a sure-fire way of ensuring that people of different backgrounds will be at cross-purposes, all assuming they know God and the mind of God. Both personal and cultural associations are conjured up like genies from particular religious lamps, to launch into battle in the mind-field which opens up. On the world-stage today the battle of religious banners wielded like blows has both primitive vehemence, and an astonishing naiveté—astonishing in the context of an otherwise highly sophisticated material society in the West. In my view, religious understanding has languished a long way behind technological understanding.

Yet underneath the rhetoric, the campaigns, the physical and ideological violence, human hearts are cowering in some confusion, longing to be understood, longing for God to declare Himself, longing to be certain; longing, indeed, for 'God'.

When I set out to know what I was dealing with, it turned up in an unexpected package. As for God, I felt I was at least on the right track, because Glyn 'knew somewhat.' I didn't know *what* he knew, but I knew *that* he knew, and how stupid would you be to turn away from that? A presence walked with him, behind the flat-footed gait and luminous eyes. It peeked out sometimes like a swirl of mystery, when he talked about the night sky, for instance and you knew he could somehow see its origin. When he mentioned the Creator, and the long lineage of Knowledge and those who had pursued it as brothers and sisters, they came alive and thronged round the edges of the room.

We were part of that lineage, a struggling part, but was Knowledge ever easy? Was God?

---

1. Appendix III, *The Last Supper – Leaving Melbourne*

Chapter 4

Leaf

Meditation is widely accepted as an essential tool for personal change and transformation, but there are many variants. A look at the nature of Meditation and the way we practised it.

"Like a leaf falling on to water. It sinks, this way, that way, descending…" he said, making a gentle drifting movement with his hand to illustrate the leaf sinking.

That was a description of how the mind stills. Not a suppression of activity, nothing sudden. No brutal engagement and no emotion. Just following the leaf which has its own destiny, its own meeting with the eternal stream below as it engages with the density of the air and the currents of wind on its inevitable journey to the source. For the leaf it means the great cycle of decay and generation, but what is the source of this great cycle, and all the cycles of decay and generation we meet with daily?

That image stayed in my mind through all the years of meditation practice, of grabbing the time to meditate in a busy life, of the times when it was a joy to settle quietly into the peace of the evening, and the times when the mind was caught unstoppably in a frenzy of 'other-things-I-should-be-doing', or the head was thick with flu, or the emotions running high with excitement or dull with depression. I understood that meditation was not an accessory to life, to be fitted in when I could, but *central.* It was the driver and carriage, and I the passenger, grateful to have discovered a means of locomotion towards a goal I trusted, however long it took, and by whatever route the logic of the undertaking demanded.

Because I certainly did not know the route. I had lots of fanciful ideas, mostly designed to keep me comfortable and cut down on effort, but fortunately, due largely to a shrewd and insightful traveller in the shape of Glyn who knew that all roads do not lead to Rome, I stuck to the route suggested.

Daily life with meditation has certain characteristics. Routine for one. Half an hour twice a day is difficult to achieve without a firm intention to set up a pattern. From the time my children were babies I used to get up half an hour earlier than they did, and trained them to stay in their cots or beds with lots of toys and books until I appeared. They took to this routine quite happily. Later in the day had to be more flexible, but there were always times when they were occupied and could understand that Mummy was meditating and not to disturb, or there might be time in the evening instead of a bit of television.

Twice a day is the ideal to maintain consistency. The effect was noticeable if you missed a few sessions or a day: a little energy dissipated. It was a little harder to sit down next time. Something was missing, a subtle quality to the day, to life.

Essence of meditation

So, what's it all about, this meditating? There are many descriptions in spiritual literature ranging from dry analysis to florid encounters with deity-figures. Add to this the socialization of meditation as a relaxing health adjunct or therapy, and the popular definition is as wide as anyone chooses to make it. Glyn was unyielding when it came to basic principles and attitude. Primary when it came to attitude was *'Don't look for results'*, which cuts out most of the above, so I had better explain why I personally found this rationale quite acceptable, even inspiring.[1]

There are not many things we do for nothing's sake. Even in philanthropic or charitable acts there are underlying benefits usually hidden somewhere in the motivation, personal gains even as simple as the warm glow of having helped someone. Nothing wrong with a warm glow—it lubricates the heart and makes further acts of giving more likely, and it doesn't need a psychologist to point out that happiness is linked to giving and selflessness. And happiness is the goal of human life—is it not?

Not on Glyn's agenda, and not on mine. By and large I was content as a child; I had no reason to be otherwise, unlike many of my less fortunate fellow human beings, so the pursuit of happiness wasn't a driving force for me. The pursuit of God, or knowledge of the real driving force behind creation, definitely was. I remember clearly sitting in front of an art-deco dressing table as the Australian sun poured through the bedroom window and wondering what the price of my being so happy and contented would be—one day. That there would be a price I never doubted; I just hoped it wouldn't be having my children slaughtered in front of me or some other such brutal horror as my young imagination conjured up. (Perhaps by Communists. Reds under the bed was the paranoia of the times). I was right in my grasp of universal economics—no free lunch—but the price was not so much brutal, as sustained and subtle. Devastation comes in many forms; but that was all to come.

However, I did accept the discipline of meditation as part of the down payment towards the debt. It was not only the magnetic field surrounding Glyn which clearly provided a foretaste of mysteries behind the mundane, but the simple logic of the process of meditating.

As Glyn presented it, the essence of meditation is the engagement and holding of a mental object, which can be a sound, image or movement like walking. As the mind stays with this object it gradually magnetises all the mental movements, flurries of thought and feelings, associative chattering etc. towards a single vector, rather like iron filings turning in one direction. And so random thought activity tends to die down, and settle, not so much round, as *near* the object, which itself gets finer and finer as does the breath. The seed-object can disappear, or hover on the edge of awareness, and pure consciousness rests within itself "like fine wine upon its lees".

This is the silence so often talked about, a silence not of absence of sound, but of a rich almost vibrating emptiness. The emptiness of Sunyata, Ku, of Ain-soph, no-thing, the naught, the void from which creation arises. Glyn often referred to it as the Unconditioned. '*Nothingness is the ground between the stars*,' he said once. But the silence itself is not the end; it is a beginning of a life lived in awareness.

Well, surely that constitutes a 'result', and one which has been extolled in every tradition worth its salt since written records began? But the paradox of its achievement is that it cannot be 'achieved', not by any Bighead out to get the benefits of wisdom, power, peace or any other goal. It took me years to realise that 'not looking for results' didn't mean there would be no results, only that *looking for* them would subvert the process, which is by nature open-ended. The results are a by-product, so to speak, of looking beyond them.

I remember a story of a seeker hoping to meet the King, who was so beguiled by the riches and pleasures of all the rooms in the palace he had to pass through on his way that of course he forgot about the King and settled for one of the 'mansions' en route. If you seek peace, or joy, or even enlightenment, you will be working toward a result: an image, a conception of what peace, joy or enlightenment might mean. It is an unavoidable consequence of the mind's operation.

So, the carrot offered was the possibility of going beyond the ordinary operation of the mind by means of practice which aims at a state of pure consciousness, a state natural to us, from which actions arise as and when necessary. From Glyn the message was that the search for meaning is just a beginning. '*There is always further to go,*' beyond meaning into the Unconditioned. '*Seek the silent ground from which meaning arises.*'

The pursuit of Nothing may not float everyone's boat, which is why so many alternative activities are offered in the name of meditation. For me and my fellows in the Work, knowing what is at the root of creation had irresistible appeal, and I think it would also resonate for many who are side-tracked into limited personal goals by the seductive promises of sellers in the meditation market. The hunger for the Limitless could be at the root of much contemporary restlessness, angst and suffering, because the twenty-first century has no name either for the hunger, or for the Limitless. It is too easy to subvert the impulse towards self-transcendence into health fetishes, extreme exploits and naked ambition, and commandeer God, the divine and the sacred into alternative ways for people to earn an income. Largely, I think we have just forgotten the height of the Highest.

Personal goals are not a crime though, and are useful. It may seem disingenuous to claim that anyone starts anything for the expectation of no reward, as it could be pointed out that that expectation is itself a reward. There are personal hopes, desires, expectations, however subtle or noble, behind every action. We are driven by desire, as the Buddha and other great spiritual teachers proclaim. Desire is attraction; without it we wouldn't get out of bed. But there is an end to desire, and it is possible to get out of bed and to act from a different source of motivation, once we have tasted and established it.

In Chapter three I described spontaneous 'slippages' occurring at intervals throughout my life, and I think these kinds of unsought events are not all that unusual. They seem to me simple evidence that it is a natural function of human psychology to be able to act from a different locus of consciousness from the one habitually used, and the mystery is why we can't manage it more often. These taster-experiences are never quite forgotten though they may be stored somewhere with other miscellaneous experiential items which don't yet add up to a whole picture. So, a bit of spontaneous experience, plus the clear, strong taste of something rich and strange provided by the person of Glyn, and finally, the logic of the process I gleaned from my readings and study were all part of the motivation for me to take meditation seriously.

I should say, however, that meditation as a practice really needs to be supported by other angles of inner work if the aim is more than to produce a state of relaxation. Indeed, whatever need underlies the search for 'relaxation' would also be better supported by a wider base of life philosophy and practice.

However, the full potential of meditation is inseparable from an integrated philosophy and metaphysic to give an overview and framework, along with other supporting practices and disciplines, such as those traditionally provided in a religious context. The context Glyn helped to establish also covered all those areas, so although some of us didn't get the distinction, the work we pursued was in essence 'religious'. It was not, however, a religion.

I began my journey in the Work without any particular bias for or against institutional religion, aware of its faults, but drawn by the inherent wisdom in any and all of the religious traditions. Somehow it was no surprise either, to find that religion did not have a monopoly on God or religious practices. How could that possibly be the case in a global age when it is possible to see the riches in so many different religious approaches? Glyn demonstrated in his person and through his activities that the Divine is not containable in any one package, and new ways of approach are possible.

To sustain a meditation practice over time, fellow travellers are an enormous help in all kinds of ways. If friends came to stay, it was accepted that at some point morning and evening they would ask for a space where they could go to meditate. It was routine; not some specialist affectation; just part of the daily pattern, and sometimes the daily pattern is one of the hardest aspects for a new meditator to establish. 'What, *every* day? *Twice…?!*' I would explain to a proto-meditator that habits and routines are very economical of energy, which is why we all have so many! Once set up, a habit runs itself. However, setting up such a counter-stream pattern is the first, maybe the greatest challenge for someone aspiring to meditate in a contemporary western lifestyle.

Courses

As well as establishing a daily rhythm, weekend retreats and longer courses with a group are helpful, perhaps indispensable from time to time. A residential retreat gives a boost of collective energy and insight, not only through the joint energies of the group, but also as a product of the pain and endurance the longer time spans and restrictions call forth. With higher and finer energy come higher and finer states of awareness. There's no mystery about this. With finer levels of awareness, a different kind of knowledge is possible, and experience deepens.

On a course or retreat, it always takes a bit of time to settle into the rhythm. By Day three I find the rhythm is starting to create space internally, but my back is starting to ache low down, or my knees, so I try to work out what can help. I try a kneeling posture, or a different chair. Perhaps just a little more tilt of the cushion? Or is it my hands dragging my shoulders down? After lunch is a killer. The sun has warmed the room, the odd bee wanders in, a few flies buzz at the windows, and the eyes droop. Oops! The chap next to me jerks suddenly upright from his gentle forward decline. Then it's my turn. Sinking, sinking…upright! Sinking, sinking, nod, droop…up again!

And so it goes through the whole torturous session. A gentle snore from the other side of the room. Blessed release when the gong sounds, and perhaps a slow walking meditation in the grounds, with the breeze blowing hair untouchably across the face, a cow lowing in the distance, something tiptoeing down the arm on minute tickly feet.

The attention in walking meditation is usually on the movement of the foot in a specific way, though on occasion hand gestures were added. I've also heard of a course in which the hapless meditators were instructed to walk backwards round a frozen pond—with eyes closed! They must have been fantastic meditators! All apparently survived, but this variant has not become standard.

Or maybe after lunch is a recreational walk with *External Considering*, keeping the attention outwards and not permitting any dwelling on internal states; leaving oneself out of the picture. All senses are turned outward, but nothing is grabbed, mauled with heavy considering. Memories start up; they are not in the present, so let them go; see that tree, the fence, the dog-rose clinging, the dustbin, the squashed beetle…

Perhaps an after-lunch walk repeating an aphorism: '*Seek the singer not the sound. The singer remains when the song has gone*' or '*Where were you when the worlds began? Where are you now? Where shall you be when your one has passed away?*'[2]

By Day Seven the mind retains its stillness, the world is fresh and clear. The back still aches, after lunch is still a battle, but everything now has depth. So much clutter has fallen away, a quiet joy settles in the heart, and past and future seems all of a piece. Towards Day Twelve you know: *'That mind which is the hidden wisdom lies silent and tranquil like good wine resting in the cask'.*[3]

What about 'Enlightenment'? Should one be aiming for a great break-through, encouraged by the widespread belief that waking up or Enlightenment is more readily available nowadays (after all, we have the technology!)? Maybe there has been a change in the world psyche, but Liberation/realization/waking up does not always come with a rush, but drop by drop, distilled, as the cells and internal currents acclimatize themselves and the psyche responds. At what point does caterpillar become butterfly?

Courses aside, the basic daily half-hour sessions morning and evening are unified by holding a sound. This is the 'leaf' which descended, and I attempted with very varying degrees of success in any given session, to follow with my attention. The instructions were clear and simple; too simple to be easy. The system Glyn devised had its origin in the ancient methodology of the Sepher Yetsirah, a Jewish text, but re-formulated into a system which for general purposes worked with three 'letters' or sounds, vowel sounds particularly chosen because they are common to almost every language. Visual and moving forms of the same system were often utilised on courses, or as most suitable for some people.

Sound, Glyn maintained, was the most penetrating route into depth, just as it is the last sense to close down at death. The sound given to each person at their initiation, was generally a combination of the three basic vowel-sounds, and it was repeated internally with the attention lightly following. It was important not to force the sound or try to direct its movement or placement, or self-will entered, and the process was no longer open-ended. You do not so much repeat the sound as *'seek within the silence another repetition.'*

The sound itself would then gradually subside with the lessening of mental activity. '*Follow. Just follow with the attention*'. It matters what sound you use though. You *could* repeat "sausage" but unless you were very skilled at avoiding all the associations which spring up with every meaningful word in a language, you would probably arrive at some celestial barbecue. The same goes for any other word. Why make it hard for yourself repeating "Love" or other concept to which you feel an allegiance or attraction, when you will have to fight through a jungle of naturally occurring lifelong associations you have built up about love before there would be any chance of entering into a concept-less, limitless space of no-thing?

This, I think, was Glyn's logic, and that of many ancient masters of the art of meditation. So we used sound without previous associations. Mental associations spring up like bindweed all over the mindscape without any extra importation at the outset!

I meditated whenever possible in a quiet room, at home, on holiday, in sickness and in health, in church, office or broom-cupboard. If no quiet room is available, a noisy one will do, provided one is not disturbed by intrusions. Noise need not be an intrusion. Meditating in the garden, however, defeated me. All my senses were tickled by every rustle, chirp, breeze, sting, and ray of sun, and my emotional being headed for 'blissed out' the instant I closed my eyes on the beauties of nature. I found it even harder work keeping attention on the sound within!

So, what are the results of seeking no results?

In those around me I saw steadiness; fragmented and unstable personalities become stable and focused; respect and tolerance for others grow with the realisation of how hard it is to be unattached to the flux and upheavals of living. I saw worldviews expanding to encompass perspectives which bred understanding; people who lived off their feelings become able to think and evaluate with clarity; intellectuals get out of some narrow mind prison and learn to appreciate the emotional power of the abstract and attend to human values and feelings. I saw hunched, nervous bodies learn to hold themselves straight, and with the development of a centre from which to look out at the world, eyes which could hold your gaze without masking some personal agenda or trying to manipulate.

All good. But meditation of this kind is not a little pill to be taken in quest of exotic experience. Experience comes in due course, and altered states of consciousness are no longer so exotic after many years sustained meditation. They have their place, and fortunately Glyn offered guidance as to what that place is. He also had some interesting advice for dealing with powerful experiences, including those spontaneous visions which have great emotional charge and are apt to carry people away: *"Put it in your forget-ory"*, he would say. In the forget-ory they would be safe, there when you need them, but not messed with and taken into your personal display cabinet, or tempting with delusions of grandeur.

The other guiding principle for meditation, as well as applying to any other aspect of inner work, was repeatedly expressed as '*There's always further to go*'. This principle comes in handy when you've located a delicious internal space and aim for it every meditation session. Or when all kinds of pyrotechnics occur in the body-spatial distortions, energies coursing through unfamiliar channels, blockages and enlivenings; or when colours, sounds, or beings appear, and you are visited with profound insights. Because all these things, and more, can arise with the sustained attention of meditation, it is vital to have someone more experienced than yourself to report to regularly, who will remind you that 'there is always further to go'. Reporting back is a facility which is available in most serious meditation systems.

High Peak Meditation

We established a network of checking under the name of High Peak Meditation[4], and everyone who was initiated was instructed that a necessary part of the process would be to present themselves for a check on a regular basis. However, as with every aspect of the Work, it was the individual's responsibility to do so. In years of introducing people to the practice, I found that this requirement was the single best guarantee of who would continue and who would let it drop, often quite quickly after the initial enthusiasm.

Checking not only supports the determination and will to continue, it steers a course through the kinds of 'phenomena' which some people more than others are prone to experience. A person's own predilections, sensitivities and mental /emotional balance naturally enter into the process, and it is simply a fact that a potentially powerful practice like meditation can upset the psychological apple-cart, and valuable experience needs to be sorted from delusion as soon as possible. What is more, inner perception needs to be refined, drawn out, trained, and that is well-nigh impossible to do for oneself. The classic spiritual literature can help. I remember being astonished when obscure writings of this genre suddenly started to make sense. To all descriptions of states or phenomena anyone encounters, applying the guideline *there's always further to go* neither devalues the useful ones, nor encourages resting with the delusional.

Seriously delusion-prone meditators, by which I mean either psychologically unbalanced, or with a burning achievement goal, or who 'know' all about meditation and are determined to 'do-it-their-way', are a problem best gently dissuaded from taking it on at the beginning, for this kind of meditation is unlikely to help their well-being.

But we all start with at least some small hand-luggage of delusion belonging to the human condition. *Freedom*, under many names and metaphorical descriptions such as enlightenment, illumination, moksha, nirvana, kensho, realization, metanoia, satori, and to whatever degree it is experienced, is a great turning-point. Among the many great and good teachers on the world-stage, I think only some few have truly made the turning which, aside from the exigencies of living in a body, sloughs off the human condition.

But what do I know? I make my way to the little summerhouse constructed at the end of my garden for meditational purposes. The summerhouse gives me and other members of the family a space away from the domestic activities so productive of pointless ruminations. It's a late luxury, not necessary to the practice, but the enclosure is a counter to the garden's distractions. In there the icy breeze of an English summer can do its worst without chilling me to the bone, the creatures of the garden can rustle and creep and the insects look for another target, while I turn toward that silence in which the Most High dwells.

I have been doing it for over forty years.

Lover, look back! When the eye turns in
And the carnival stills,
Its music and horses fled to some summer
Moving in snatches on the rim, and are gone into time,
Time is unwound and love is full.[5]

---

1. See my first book: *The Meditator's Guidebook*, Lucy Oliver, Destiny 1991
2. Appendix II : Twelve Aphorisms
3. op. cit.
4. www.highpeakmeditation.org.uk
5. Appendix III: Death and Meditation

Chapter 5

Backbone

Working and studying as a group was fundamental to our method, but often challenging. Can digital interactions replace the traditional working group? How working together can facilitate personal growth and change —general principles.

It was the usual raw London winter's night, as I left the stale rattle and sallow light of the Tube, past people wrapped in dark coats, and made my way through the square where a few last autumn leaves clung to the pavement. Then into the barn-like spaces of a public 'halls for hire', where we had a little back room tucked away up some stairs.

I was a bit late and going over what I would report as feedback about our weekly task, which I had managed to remember some of the time. Late was not good. We started on time. Before entering the room, the instruction was always to leave all the cares and concerns of the day outside, for the room was a work-space, a place set aside. I paused outside the door to let go of my preoccupations, and crept into the little circle where a short silence was already in place to help with setting the (internal) space. The silence was restful, settling, growing deeper.

After the silence came ninety minutes of vigorous discussion, feeding back the results of working with the subject for investigation, grounding it in daily life and observation, so that by the end whatever topic we had taken as the object of study for that evening was no longer an abstract concept. The results of shared work like this are cumulative and visible only over time as they integrate. We ended that meeting as usual by choosing another topic as homework for the coming week, a subject for practical investigation and observation in our own everyday life. We formally closed with another period of silence. A bit of socializing over cups of tea and coffee concluded the evening, and a collection to pay for the room.

Then I was back in the chilly night, making my way home through the city streets with food for thought and a sharpened up sensory awareness as I headed for the Underground. This was the standard pattern for face to face group work, week after week, and year after year for those who took seriously the quest for Knowledge in a tradition which was neither monastic, scholarly nor occult, but rooted in ordinary living. I'm describing a commercial venue, but regular local meetings were usually in someone's living room, with external venues mostly hired for special events or for geographical convenience.

Rules of Engagement

This kind of group work has a magical quality, which cannot be matched by individual and isolated reading or thinking, no matter how voluminous or intensive. What emerges from focused group discussion is a commonality of experience maturing from interaction with different individuals and personality types. It only happens by shifting the ground away from ego, away from personal opinions and obsessions, and the usual social personae. A working group becomes more than the sum of its parts, and the individuals within it grow and change along with the maturing understanding of the group.

However, the only way to achieve this kind of operation is by establishing certain agreed conditions or rules, and every individual doing his or her best to observe them, no matter how passionate the discussion becomes. Passion is generally in partnership with 'opinion' rather than observation, and in order to allow fresh ideas and perspectives with the potential for genuinely transformative shifts, a rule like *Neither Accepting nor Rejecting* leaves space for the new to enter.

However, it is a difficult practice to follow. Even if we manage to curb our immediate rejection of an idea which is not in accord with our previous thinking, curbing the impulse to embrace and accept a congenial position seems positively unnatural! Only if you try it out will you see that by neither accepting nor rejecting, you are creating a gap of awareness, from which choice can be made, or a much wider picture start to emerge. Creating such gaps is fundamental to the work of consciousness and to sustaining a *working group*—not a social gathering nor an exchange of ideas or feelings. Assertive personalities and reticent folk alike are equally responsible for upholding the group's aim of *Knowledge is not information*, hence the instruction to 'leave at the door' your personal agenda, as well as all the preoccupations of the day just gone. However, personality is not left at the door, so there is plenty of opportunity for the practice of forbearance and respect for others, and no lack of grit to form a few pearls!

Our groups were vigorous and robust in discussion, and without a teacher. A programme of work or study can be facilitated by anyone taking the role as Chair, providing there is organised material and some guidelines or precepts to act as an essential backbone for the growth of a Knowledge body. Hence, we had Rules of Discipline, ('discipline' meaning voluntary self-discipline, not strictures imposed from without).

SPEAK AND ACT ONLY AS NECESSARY
DO NOT CRITICISE (EVEN ONESELF)
NEGATIVE EMOTIONS ARE NEVER NECESSARY
ACTIVE INVESTIGATION
EXTERNAL CONSIDERING
NEITHER ACCEPT NOR REJECT
SPEAK FROM EXPERIENCE
REFINE OBSERVATION
REMEMBER THE BREATH
KNOWLEDGE IS NOT INFORMATION

These are practices, not moral dictates or good thoughts. I will expand briefly on a few to set the scene, but they are designed for argument and dialogue, not for exposition with a fixed interpretation. 'Rules' is probably a misnomer.

For example, to *externally consider* you must consciously and deliberately turn your attention *outwards* to the situation you are in, while turning off the incessant inner commentary, which is your own internal thinking and opinions about it. By doing this, the normal flow of 'me-centred' rumination is checked, and in its absence, you are in a position to *refine your observation* and act effectively.

In any context, the recommendation to *speak from experience* is relevant, but particularly in a group it facilitates striving for honesty and deeper engagement. Most ordinary conversation and discussion rely on previous information and secondary sources; in other words what we've heard, read, or been told by someone (*their* experience). We need this kind of information to navigate life, but for the aim of self-knowledge, only that which has been acted upon, integrated and is genuinely your *own* observation is a learning experience for self and others. One can often recognise beliefs and opinions by the vehemence and passion with which they are asserted.

Is it true that *negative emotions are never necessary?* What, *never?* —as you reflect upon all the perfectly legitimate causes of suffering in this life.

Irrespective of the cause provoking it, you can look and see what is happening *in you* in a state of negativity, and then ask yourself if it is possible to take a corrective action, or to criticize, without the accompaniment of negative feelings. Is there a difference between grief and negativity? What does *negative* actually mean to your organism, in your psyche? And then you can ask whether emotion with this tonality achieves anything material, other than wasting a lot of energy and completely suffusing your vision, and in fact, causing you to suffer? What is routinely squandered in emotion may not be obvious without closer investigation. The fashionable epidemic of 'taking offence' is murderous to the wellbeing of individuals as well as to the social fabric.

So how do we judge what's necessary? *Speak and act only as necessary* sounds as if it might preclude ninety per cent of human communication and action, especially if it includes not speaking when we should speak, withholding a useful contribution in discussion, or keeping silent instead of defending someone or something. I remember a lesson at the age of 12 when I heard a bunch of smart and popular girls mocking my new desk-mate. I was very clearly aware at the time, that not only was I not speaking up in her defence, but I was sorely tempted to burnish my own credentials by joining in. My own judgement and my good-will towards her definitely wavered. But recognising this contagion, *seeing* it, transformed cowardice into a moment of Knowledge, whose influence has stayed with me through fifty years. It was just a moment, but one with power. Every discipline of the Work, and all these rules, are aimed at making it possible for more of these life-transforming quiet, grey nano-seconds of awareness to arise.

The concept of *Necessity* as a guiding principle has roots in antiquity, appearing in Plato's Republic as the Spindle of Necessity (we will return to this myth in later chapters). One of the aspects of the story is a lesson about choice under the rule (throne) of Necessity, as souls between lives chose their new life and destiny. Only those souls who had suffered in previous lives used their experience to choose wisely, perhaps because they had learned to recognise what is truly necessary. Necessity is not at all obvious; it really puts you on the spot. It might mean pausing before action, reflecting on the necessity or otherwise, whereupon you would also have the clarity to report precisely and in detail when sharing this moment of observation with others.

Sharing is helpful, because hearing another person's description may arouse a resonance in you, and suddenly your own experience and memory is awakened. Your own intuitions, perhaps only half-felt and discarded. A fleeting sense of significance. Observations which don't quite cohere. All such transitory impressions can acquire *mass* once you re-cognise them through someone else's description, for they are your experience too. Much of the value of working with a group is to do with recognition, pulling forth your own experience from the darkness of your unawareness of it. Like the miller's daughter in Rumpelstiltskin, you can spin internal straw into true gold on the wheel of recognition.

The Digital challenge

Times change. These dedicated working groups may seem less relevant in a globally connected world, when spiritual and esoteric teachings are readily available through the internet. Once closely guarded secret rituals are secret no longer, (though secrecy for secrecy's sake was never the point.) Wide and diverse opportunities for spiritual work are dominated by 'satsangs' with recognised Teachers, lectures and talks either live or online, interactive webinars and remote meetings, supported by occasional more intensive workshops or retreats which cost a lot to attend. However, apart from meditation groups, the type of ongoing study group I've been describing—face to face regular working together—might be harder to find, but I think there is a sense in which it is irreplaceable.

It would be antediluvian not to embrace and exploit new ways of interacting, bringing people together right across the globe, and increasing the range of possibilities and exposure to teachings. Yet, 'teachings' are a small part of the journey towards self-knowledge. Reputedly, some of the wisest, enlightened beings throw away their books, sutras, writings when finally, they *know*. Group work is like a mirror—you really learn to see yourself, recognise your strengths and weaknesses, and make philosophy relevant and functional in your own life.

As the internet becomes increasingly a dispenser of wisdom, a new kind of pan-global institution serving spirituality, there is a need to weigh up and re-assess what is happening, and what the effects are. All human institutions are subject to mission-creep and adulteration, from sheer proliferation, from time and habit, from the mixed motivations of participants and organisers, and in response to the natural Law of Octaves and its interval points which will be explained in Chapter 7.[1] There are considerable gains from our digital connectedness, but it is timely to ask if anything important is being lost.

For instance, can the impact and force of the natural Field which is created between people in physical proximity be replicated in cyber-space? What is *lost* without actual face to face contact? Perhaps the gleam in an eye? Or the finer signals of body language, and the ability to work the subtle substance of an energetic aura, or weave the polarised field between beings? These skills are the tools of a genuine spiritual master and a fundamental art in wisdom teaching. As every seeker who finds such a master knows, it is potent simply to sit in the presence of realised human Being. A resonance phenomenon occurs, and teaching or transmission can happen without a word being spoken.

As we utilise the benefits of the internet, how do we ensure that the real is not lost in the virtual, and the true jewel not overtaken by glassy replication? Is it enough simply to recognise and name the danger? From my own experience, online communication relies largely on *verbal* information, and is too slow and cumbersome for the darting response which can pick up a thread from another's words and tug it productively. Sometimes screen-to-screen communication feels to me like a tennis match between hippopotamuses—backwards and forwards, serve and receive, keep to your side, cover the court… The dragonfly of the spirit has a hard time operating!

A 'working' group is a formal structure by virtue of which an energy field is generated and sustained, empowering and energising individuals and mutually supporting and motivating each person in it. These are human engagement factors in action. Together the participants learn to understand each other with an agreed terminology and framework so as to disentangle the varied associations people have with words and concepts. Words, concepts, verbal information and descriptions, even teachings, are not *reality*. They need unpicking before they can be properly integrated, and that takes a bit of time.

Also, in contrast to the ease of a podcast or webinar in your own home, there is no firmer foundation than the sheer effort of will engaged by going out of your comfort zone every week on a cold winter's evening, after a day at work, whether you feel like it or not. Armchair spirituality it is not.

And then there is the issue of money, reward, profit. Glyn was adamant that in service of the Work, not a penny was to be taken for personal gain. It is the material analogue of the principle of *no personal profit,* and inviolable. There was occasionally an argument that "people don't value what they get for nothing, so we should charge a little", but it was easy to sense the thin end of a wedge, and once the way to Knowledge becomes a profit-making commodity, it changes everything, on every level, and alters the nature of the Work. So, we covered expenses, but no aspect of the Work was an income-earner for anyone, and this remains an essential principle.

But it also kept us small, and again the Internet has opened a new can of worms—sheer scale, proliferation of materials and participants, and a huge increase in the potential reach. Then there's the PR factor of presentation, and the seductiveness of charisma. Glyn warned constantly about the illusory nature and danger of charisma, nipping it in the bud if ever he saw it developing in someone, which is partly why he was always edgy to be around. However, there are no checks on these factors online.

We are now the beneficiaries of a rich heritage of texts in translation making their way into general global spirituality from diverse cultures and traditions. The general availability of such a cornucopia of original and ancient sources is a new phenomenon, and it does have consequences. For instance, what is appropriate practice or expectation in the original context may not be particularly helpful in a modern way of life, even if the root insights are universally valid. Whilst being divorced from their cultural setting and praxis and available to anyone at whatever level of understanding is not necessarily a problem, it can be an excess of riches, and do more to obfuscate than clarify a way forward for a particular person looking for practical guidance.

Also, it is not often acknowledged or recognised that much of the revered spiritual literature in all traditions has arisen in, and is geared towards a *monastic way of life*, itself closely bound up with culture and period. The differences between a monastic specialist environment and aiming for the same development in the conditions of ordinary life 'in the world' are quite deep-rooted. I was taken aback attending a retreat from a different tradition to realize there was an overt assumption that the path of 'real' practice, for those who are genuinely serious, involves years of solitary practice, sessions of eleven hours without a break, years of studying under other 'world-class' teachers, and learning the practice of a gymnastic repertoire of mental observations. Clearly no hope at all for me then, or for the other lay-schmucks along for a temporary ride!

The underlying assumption that a monastic path is the 'best' is rarely questioned among religious professionals, and it is misleading, not because there isn't value in circumstances which make it possible to concentrate so totally, but for two ancillary reasons. One is because the very intensity of concentration generates its own specialist problems which in turn generate specialist solutions and advice (in the literature); and secondly, because living in the world can lead in the same direction—just with a different set of problems, activities and therefore advice needed.

Do both lead to the same *end*? Posed as a koan, the answer is probably yes and no, and begs the question: What *end* are you looking for?

'Our path is for generalists,' said Glyn. It's a true challenge because there is no supporting environment to hold one to it, and everything around is pulling in the opposite direction. Instead of seclusion in a monastery high in the mountains, we just had Glyn's kitchen as a point of reference. He rarely attended local group meetings except as a guest visit by invitation, but he presided from the kitchen, always interested to hear what was going on, and always ready to debate any point of theory. If the groups were the backbone, our own efforts and lives put on muscle. But if we lost our way, grew flabby or despondent, a visit to the kitchen would restore the realization that common everyday living is not a barrier to the Highest.

Group Dynamics

He once visited us in Oxford and made a circuit of everyone seated round in a group meeting, standing before each person for a few minutes and then touching each person lightly on or near either head or chest. This looked like an unaccustomed exercise in some sort of magic. He stood in front of me and brought his hand to my chest. Immediately there was a burning sensation, a powerful localised heat which penetrated and made my heart literally *burn* within me. I was too bemused to ask afterwards what this uncharacteristic display was all about.

People came and went through the individual groups and Saros, but throughout the Eighties a consistent core averaging probably about sixty people across the country was formed. Initially, there was a predominance of young university educated types, but also a fair sprinkling of others. We were geographically dispersed, because from the centres of Oxford, Cambridge, London and Manchester, people from these university towns eventually migrated to other parts, leaving London and Manchester as the main foci. Glyn's Kitchen was a magnet for any one visiting London.

However, in Oxford, for instance, the group was not purely university based, but drew on Town as well as Gown. The Town contingent included a willowy left-over Hippie with long-hair and an interest in herbs (the medicinal variety mainly; the other sort was not encouraged as incompatible with the aims of clarity) whom we called Herbie Sam. He was accompanied by his mate John, a wiry, bespectacled individual of no very fixed abode or employment. Herbie Sam drifted in and out over the years, but John stuck. He drove about on three wheels in a frequently overloaded Reliant Robin, which demanded a powerful exercise of faith in Something from those who drove in it. Over the years John gained in stature, almost physically. He matured into a steady husband and father, managing a charity, becoming a skilled photographer, and maintaining an intelligent dedication to the Work. He was much missed when he succumbed to a lung disease contracted from his job, at an unseemly early age.

Many years later I ran a group in my home in London, similar but not identical to the format described earlier in this chapter. This one became very stable after a time—too stable in my view. It had become a comfortable sociable night out! Nothing wrong with affection and good conversation—the bonds of friendship generated through group work are deep—but I felt it was my duty to try and keep the edge, as it became plain that some of the participants were taking the Work aspect a bit lightly. First, I moved the meeting into another room and launched into a drier theoretical phase, which caused a few rumbles of complaint. They had become attached to the space of the front room, and weren't keen on 'theory'.

They mostly survived that phase, but gladly returned to the status quo when it finished. Next, I tried asking each of them to spend the six weeks' break over Christmas brushing up on some religious/spiritual system they were not familiar with and give a ten-minute presentation to the group as their contribution rather than mine. Very reasonable I thought, as well as educative. But to my surprise it engendered some outright refusal mixed with 'too busy', 'I can't' and other expressions of reluctance. Where was the Work ethos of responsibility and effort? Some participants took the challenge, learned a lot from doing it, and stimulated a series of interesting and informative meetings in the new year.

But I was determined to shake out the slothful. Closing the group would not necessarily be a learning experience for anyone, so instead I organised some help to run a twelve-week ritual course at an outside venue on a different weekday evening, and made attendance at all twelve the condition for participating. As I suspected, some were not prepared for this commitment, and thereby missed a very valuable and moving experience which has not been repeated. The course was called 'Twelve Gates into the City' and each week's session took as a theme one archetypal activity essential to life in the mythological City of the World, roles like Teacher, Merchant, Architect etc. The principles behind each archetype were explored through discussion and group exercises and then collectively enacted in a ritual. As I will elaborate in a later chapter, the drama of ritual teaches without words, using the body and symbolic objects as a language to ground insight and shift perception.

Impressions

I have emphasised the more rigorous aspects of group work in this chapter to preserve awareness of this route, even as the tide of change presents other opportunities and inducements, emphasizing reward but not always offering method. Freedom and restriction are the wheels of this vehicle. People tend to envisage transcendental raptures when beginning the path, and may even be gifted with such a taste early on, but actually, the more prosaic task of saving energy and learning how to transform it through observation and self-knowledge is the only reliable instrument to shift cognition, and lead to gnosis, illumination, wisdom, or peace which is stable and lasting. Thanks to the stimulus and guidance of group working, even a lazy individual like myself, with High Ambition but no idea how to go about realising it, can strengthen the psychic backbone.

Just as breathing in air with all its component gases is necessary fuel for the physical body's processes, so the *impressions* absorbed from the outside world provide fuel for the growth of other inner 'bodies'.[2] The quality of the fuel/food is dependent on the degree of conscious attention given to the impressions which enter through the senses. Holidays automatically refresh us with a feast of new impressions, but a walk down the street with *external considering* also generates new impression-food for a jaded or depressed soul, perhaps lifting the spirit a little. To be clear, it's not just the walk, it's the attention which makes the difference. Mundane as it sounds, how we process impressions is at the core of esoteric work, along with the ability to conserve the energy we routinely waste in negativity. *Negative emotions are never necessary.* The group is actually a kind of laboratory for the refinement of impressions.

Four worthwhile aims for Generalists defined by Glyn:

To be able to recognise Truth wherever it may be. (He suggested you 'hear' with the back of the head if something has 'truth' in it).
To help people to live with themselves.
To be able to look at Immensity without being frightened.
To gain a deeper appreciation of identity beyond social identity.

---

1. See Chapter 7 for an explanation of Octave Theory
2. eg. Hinduism – Five Sheaths; Tibetan Buddhism three kayas; subtle energy bodies

Chapter 6

Lines

When asked to explain the origins of our approach and training I always have a problem, and grow a bit shifty. There is no authorized version to reach for or packaged lineage to offer as a handle for the (admittedly few) people who are bothered to ask about it seriously. A further problem is the explosion of consciousness studies, worldviews, contemplative courses, psychological and parapsychological research, quantum, epigenetic, cosmological advances— all with a bearing on human experience and view of reality. It looks like a lot of choice if your aim is Knowledge.

The one unifying factor in the field of consciousness studies and research, whether approaching from a medical, psychological, pure science or spiritual angle, is that there is no unifying factor—yet. At the present time there is intense interest but absolute diversity, from which not even those approaches designating themselves 'integral' escape. Some are more inclusive than others, some philosophical, some experimental, some mutually contradictory, some materialistic, and others in which consciousness is the primal originating force, the cause of all creation and evolution.

An esoteric approach means working from the inside outwards, identifying principles which are hidden unless you look for them. It's not that principles are somehow 'pre-existent' forms. They are, like every concept, a product of the 'looking', of the human ability to slice the cake of reality into intelligible measures which can satisfy the need for meaning. But we also know there is a process, a learning curve to become familiar with anything. Consciousness is an inside-out subject if ever there was one, and the word *esoteric* takes on its full meaning of inner and hidden.

In everyday speech we use esoteric to mean obscure or reserved for a select few. In this sense the *esoteric* side of the scientific discipline is closed to me personally; I've not been trained for it, and accept the fact that a whiteboard covered with equations is beyond my grasp, (not helped by the lecturer in one science-related subject I once studied, whose habit was to write with one hand and erase with the other as he progressed across the board. It certainly kept the board tidy!)

The need for training, which we accept readily in the arena of material science, applies even more so to the mysteries of consciousness, whether approached from the outside (in a laboratory) or from the inside (e.g. in my front room!). Esoteric knowledge and training go together, and there is always an element of oral transmission in authentic, living knowledge. The oral, by definition, simply can't be captured when written down. It joins up the dots of the written products. Oral transmission imparts the human interaction, the dynamic, the energy behind it, and perhaps something more mysterious still, something behind the spoken word. The ultimate questions about life and consciousness open to an esoteric approach, and have always been best served by person to person transmission.

Glyn's quest for this kind of esoteric knowledge in the 1950's and 60's found him selling books down the Charing

Cross Road, and attending astrological groups in the new Soho Coffee Bars where the trendy and eccentric would hang out. Post-war Soho was a seedy place of strip-clubs, coffee-bars and corrupt policemen, and London in the Beatnik era was a city in recovery from the major trauma of the war. Even in the 70's when I knew it, the streets of London were comparatively empty, and cars circulated round Leicester Square, which is now a heaving cosmopolitan mass of pedestrian precinct. In Leicester Square I ate my first roasted chestnuts from a chestnut-vendor with a little brazier burning in the frosty air, and first heard a nightingale sing as the evening sank into the square.

Pavement cafés were unknown then: after all, who would want to sit outside in the dismal chill of a London winter? People's tolerance must have changed because the weather hasn't! Watkins Bookshop was the heart of esoteric reading. I visited it every time I came down from Oxford, looking for the gems of wisdom which would enthral my evenings. Then I ate falafel in a little café around the corner, engrossed in my latest purchase or ruminating on the mythological impact of Star Wars, which I saw two Fridays in a row. Watkins is still there, but the books are glossier and the other esoteric bookshops competing with it are long closed down. Tottenham Court Road is no longer the same mecca for the second-hand book browser.

When I compare what I read then, and my current voluminous reading on all subjects relating to consciousness from every angle which Amazon supplies to my door, I am deeply grateful for those few tatty books which passed from hand to hand, the torn sheets of paper with diagrams and his latest analysis of the human condition which Glyn would thrust at you, and the hours of puzzling over them and copying which followed.

I am grateful because in principle, 'knowledge', even without the capital K, doesn't come from sheer volume and is not the same as 'information', no matter how much information you absorb. There is an issue of depth, of integration. If you truly 'know' something, it is part of you and you can find many and varied ways to express or employ it, depending on context and circumstances. Moreover, and of paramount importance in Glyn's teaching, is that '*Knowledge cannot be passed on, but only the way to knowledge*'; that is, the method by which one can reach it.

Information is different. It can be useful, you can collect vast quantities of it, but it doesn't imply integration, and if not passed on exactly as received, it may be inaccurate and misleading. The sea of information in our digital age has created a situation of drift, of overwhelm, and there is a real need for education to discern the difference between knowledge and information, as they serve different purposes. One of my aims in recording these notes and impressions is to convey a flavour which might help identify the essential elements of the genuine and gainful from the overabundance of information so freely available. A 'flavour' relates to tasting, which relates to 'sapiens' meaning wise.

The Poem

I'll explore the theme of *Knowledge* through Glyn's favourite poem, which he was apt to quote often, particularly the refrain and last line. It seems old-fashioned now, and always seemed to me to have a faintly quaint and archaic ring about it, but it clearly contained a message he considered important, and it also seems to capture something essential about him as a teacher and visionary. The poem is Rudyard Kipling's *The Palace*, written about the turn of the last century, and it draws on the imagery of Freemasonry which in Kipling's long and varied career as a statesman, visionary and literary figure "opened another world" for him. For Glyn, who was not a freemason, the goals, symbolism and initiate structure of masonry was part of the esoteric cosmos he was drawn to re-examine and vivify.

I have spent a lot of time puzzling over its meaning and in particular what it meant to Glyn. Leaving aside the specific allusions to historical freemasonry, the metaphor and symbolism has general relevance, and Glyn used it as a conveyance of a contemporary message, of the work he and we were engaged upon, and speaking to any spiritual, esoteric endeavour. Not so much archaic, as timeless.

When I was a King and a Mason – a Master proven and skilled –
I cleared me ground for a Palace such as a King should build.
I decreed and dug down to my levels. Presently, under the silt,
I came on the wreck of a Palace such as a King had built.

There was no worth in the fashion – there was no wit in the plan –
Hither and thither, aimless, the ruined footings ran –
Masonry, brute, mishandled, but carven on every stone:
"After me cometh a Builder. Tell him, I too have known."

Swift to my use in my trenches, where my well-planned ground-
works grew,
I tumbled his quoins and his ashlars, and cut and reset them anew.
Lime I milled of his marbles; burned it, slacked it, and spread;
Taking and leaving at pleasure the gifts of the humble dead.

Yet I despised not nor gloried; yet, as we wrenched them apart,
I read in the razed foundations the heart of that builder's heart.
As he had risen and pleaded, so did I understand
The form of the dream he had followed in the face of the thing he had planned.

* * *

When I was a King and a Mason – in the open noon of my pride,
They sent me a Word from the Darkness. They whispered and called me aside.
They said – "The end is forbidden." They said – "Thy use is fulfilled.
"Thy Palace shall stand as that other's – the spoil of a King who shall build."

I called my men from my trenches, my quarries, my wharves, and my sheers.
All I had wrought I abandoned to the faith of the faithless years.
Only I cut on the timber – only I carved on the stone:
"After me cometh a Builder. Tell him, I too have known!"

The story in summary is that following his personal ambition to construct a 'Palace', (which symbolically is any enterprise or project with a lot of personal investment), a builder who is very confident of his own skill and his own grand design, comes upon the ruins of a previous palace. To him, these ruins of someone else's dreams are rough and poorly designed, so he proceeds to salvage what he can for his own construction. But he notices that on every stone is carved some words: *"After me cometh a Builder. Tell him I too have known."*

These haunting words start to invade his consciousness and heart, and he begins to resonate in sympathy with that previous builder of long ago, the dream of another human heart. But he carries on with his own construction and re-working until a jolt comes from outside. *"They sent me a word from the darkness."*

This is the point of change. Who are "They"? Why is "the end forbidden"? Why must his palace not be completed, that he should pull it down and leave it like a remnant, a reminder of something not achieved, a warning to the future?

There are echoes here of every great shock or reversal in one's life. This builder is engaged in a perfectly legitimate pursuit, but his deeper intuition has been awoken. Hearing the voice from the darkness, he understands and heeds it, and exactly like his predecessor, he abandons his grandiose project and pulls it all down. The ruins he will leave for someone else to find one day, and in his turn, he carves on the fragments the words: *"After me cometh a Builder. Tell him I too have known."*

I like poetry, but for a long time this one didn't immediately make sense to me, nor did the importance Glyn seemed to attach to it. The metaphor is drummed in with a remorseless rhythm and lilting rhyme scheme. In the repetition of those mysterious words: *"After me cometh a Builder. Tell him I too have known,"* you can sense the march of generations and the passing down of Knowledge from one age to the next. There's a warning too, a hint of admonition, a reminder that Knowledge is not grandiose structures of thought, whether written or embodied in institutions, but is passed down the line from one person to another. The nature of *knowing* is that it can't be accumulated and stored like wealth. Only traces, the spoil remaining from people who have managed to mine the depths can be found. Knowledge is not in the palace; it is in the builder, the aware Being who is capable of hearing whispers from the darkness.

As Glyn said many times, all we can pass on is the *way* to Knowledge, not Knowledge itself. However, carving words on stone for the next comer is a duty. The Way may involve turning away from pride and ambition towards humble service, even apparent failure. How many of us setting out to plumb the mystery of the universe are expecting to achieve a 'palace' and the power implied? Or at least charisma, status, a role in an organisation we have helped to build? To pull it all down, and leave just the traces, with a message for those who come after—that is quite something!

Glyn lived unknown, virtually unphotographed, with only the footings of his own grand design left to indicate that he had Known, and under his auspices we all took down the organisation of Saros we had built over twenty years. Other great teachers have acted similarly, dismantling projects which had become ends in themselves instead of service of the Highest. The Indian Master Meher Baba shocked his followers and the community by dismantling his ashrams and hospital to take to the road and become 'helpless and hopeless'. Mother Teresa insisted that her chief work was training her Sisters, not looking after the dying. Ruthlessness is the only safeguard against the law of spiritual entropy and the creeping corruption of attachment to human goals. Compromise is never an option in these matters.

An oral tradition of knowledge may leave very few traces, but surfaces under different forms in different times and places. It ignores the boundaries of culture and religion. In what is known as the Perennial Tradition, you can see a line running through Middle Ages Christianity, Kabbalism, Sufism, the Renaissance, and preserved in esoteric teachings, glyphs and art, and also manifesting in little known groups who attempted to return to first principles, such as the Brothers and Sisters of the Common Life in northern Europe from the 14th to the 16th centuries who were the teachers of Erasmus.

The Word

Kipling's poem is like a long koan, with the meaning held under its tension. I came to see in it the reflection of Glyn and his philosophy and his own personal lack of attachment to any material thing or any product of his work or imagination. He gave all away freely. '*With any luck, someone will steal it,*' he'd say when he or anyone else came up with a good idea, or developed a useful or potent piece of theory. He wrote and collected together twelve aphorisms which were useful in a meditative context, and one of them read:

> *"Pick fruit and pass it on, the same is a service.*
> *Pick fruit and eat it, you will be asked to account for it."* [1]

I tremble slightly when I read that. I think I have eaten too much fruit.

The Word from the darkness must be that same potent creative Word as the sound used in meditation, as that which God spoke in the Book of Genesis, as the symbol which appears in many sacred scriptures including ancient Zoroastrian, and as the 'Word become flesh'. A word is a symbol and a vibration, a formation of meaning of which it has been truly said, it is more powerful than the sword. Although violence can destroy and shuffle the pieces on the world-board, civilisation arises from the steady creative force symbolised by the Word. From language and writing to the communication with a higher level of reality, Word is the hidden dynamic behind the greatest flowering of art and culture.

The Kipling poem was read at Glyn's funeral, beside the coffin over which a light grey cloak was formally but casually thrown. This cloak symbolised Knowledge for us, and was used in performances down the years such as the Turning where it swirled and billowed to the thump of the foot on the floor. So, it seemed apt that it be laid over his coffin, and a handful of long-stemmed iris were scattered over the cloak.

Irises were special to him. He once described to me an illumination produced by the sight of yellow-flag irises glimpsed en masse beside a stream. I remembered his vision much later when wandering the wide watery wastes of the Camargue, I too came upon a stream lined with yellow iris, and the empty grey skies and plains briefly flamed with gold, just as vision breaks through the ordinariness of everyday perception.

The grey cloak over the coffin had a trick in store. It was lightly thrown over, but when it came to be removed so the coffin could glide through the doors into the darkness, it refused. Caught somehow on the wood, the cloak declined to leave easily the man who had brought it into being and who had woven in diagram and action so many masterly cloaks for the Knowledge which he carried and was determined to perpetuate. It was the final glitch, the final reminder that all does not go the way we expect or want, the last interval in a process about to complete—until a hefty tug delivered the cloak into the hands of those of us remaining to perpetuate in our turn. We listened to the single sustained note of the organ as the coffin slid through the gates.

Over the drone, was there a chuckle of innocent merriment?

Faith and Belief

"The faith of the faithless years" is a phrase encapsulating the heart of Glyn's philosophy and teaching. Faith, he distinguished from '*faith in*' anything. If there is an object, the state is not faith but *belief*. You may give your heart and acceptance (*lief* – to hold dear) to some declaration or object, but is not necessarily true, however much belief you invest. Dogmas, second–hand descriptions, superstitions, even our senses and perception can be delusional. Beliefs can be founded on the purest ignorance, or represent layers accumulated over time on a basis of truth, but subject to being modulated and accruing unnecessary mass and embellishment down the years. Belief can, however, co-exist with Faith; they are just not the same thing.

Faith without an object is an attitude, a *turning towards* not dependent on any formulation. It is an instrument, an attitude of trust and confidence which, because it has roots in reality, can be maintained in the darkest conditions, in grief, imprisonment and confusion. The roots of Faith in the heart are cultivated through experience, experiment, thought, observation, and investigation. The quality of faith has no boundaries. Its transcendent nature allows it to co-exist with Doubt, a state of paradox which is not only viable, but quite important. Some Zen Buddhist teaching advocates encouraging the Great Doubt as a highly productive state of mind, producing the sort of tension which cracks koans, those riddles which can take years of dedicated frustration to penetrate.

The Builder of the poem abandoned everything to this sort of Faith alone. That he could do so, implies that through his own "faithless years" when he was preoccupied with material gains and pragmatic skills, the conditions for faith must have at least loitered within him, or he would not have even heard the Word or recognised its whisper, let alone heed it. There's reassurance for us here. The right touch, the right circumstance, or a moment of waking up can remind and stir the sleeping soul. For us all, in these apparently faithless years, in the face of a world conspiring against such intangible objectives, it takes a lot of commitment to maintain Faith.

Beliefs are easy; Faith is not.

Three Lines of Work

How to sustain Faith, when it has no tangible shape and form? Glyn's answer was *method* and being active and committed on three levels which he called the Three Lines of Work: work on self, work for others and work for the Work itself.[2]

In the first place, *Work on Self* begins with one's own 'prima materia', foundational material for the Great Work as the alchemical mythology describes it, and which consists of all the aspects of personal selfhood: faults, foibles, limitations, fears, strengths and predispositions. To avoid the side-step of personal development becoming an end in itself, merely an expression of ambition or a therapeutic need, work on self should be balanced by working *with* and *for* others in disinterested service: *Work for Others.*

The third Line, *Work for the Work* guides, inspires and subsumes the other two Lines, keeping in mind that the aim is to realize Knowledge, Wisdom and Being. For this it needs to be the whole package. Although there is a sequence of development, the third without the other two can be illusion, while without the third, the other two can amount to no more than self-interest.

Glyn led by example. His life was turned over to Faith and he never ceased to insist on its importance, even while creating for the rest of us the difficult problem of knowing what to call it in the absence of a recognisable 'brand name'. He simply embodied service. Assorted odd-bods would turn up in his kitchen at all hours of the day and night, expecting gems of wisdom to fall from his lips, or proposing half-baked schemes to transform the universe. Glyn listened patiently, turned what he could to advantage, or launched into an animated discussion of social issues which invariably turned conventional thinking on its head and challenged underlying assumptions. He expected to be argued with. He was always looking to identify the fundamental principles underlying the masks of human behaviour. '*Everyone has an agenda*,' he would say. '*Look for the hidden agenda*'.

In the early days he didn't spare himself in setting up groups and courses to further his own agenda. His agenda only became clear later. It was a non-personal dedication to serving Knowledge through his particular talents, (not—as many of us thought—to further *our* development as individuals, nor collectively to establish an organisation.) Glyn always insisted he was not a Guru, a role aimed at imparting wisdom by nurturing followers, and demonstrated it in later years by withdrawing more and more to concentrate on his abstract work, freeing us as individuals to develop his endowment with whatever talents and wisdom we could command.

For me, Work commitments had priority over other social engagements, my sense of the obligation towards a teaching which rooted itself in the everyday. In the original definition of the 'Fourth Way' by Gurdieff/Ouspensky, it differs from three more traditional Ways symbolised by Fakir (physical discipline), Monk (emotional/devotional) or Yogi (intellectual/insight), which all require some degree of retirement from the world. The Fourth Way, 'the way of the sly man' is undertaken in the midst of worldly life, and a degree of 'slyness' or careful navigation of pitfalls is indispensable.

To a person of contemplative disposition, the second Way of devotion is rather appealing though. In my young convent education, I had been deeply struck by a horror story told to us by a fat old nun about how never to reject a religious vocation if God should call us to His service. Apparently one rebellious young woman had declined to follow her "call" to be a nun and was immediately involved in a car accident. "The steering-wheel went right through her stomach!" said Mother C with lurid emphasis.

This story presented me with a dilemma. On the one hand I was determined to do my best by God, as I had no doubt it was the highest option when it came to job-choices, but on the other hand, and despite all the tales of religious life I absorbed with devout fascination, I was quite sure I did not wish to confine myself to a nunnery. Life was too rich and various, and God must be locatable and able to be served in its midst, surely? But the steering-wheel was ominous. What if God did 'call' me? Therefore, at the end of my evening prayers was a regular addendum: "…and please God, don't make me a nun."

The prayer was answered; no call came, or at least, not that I noticed. Although I have the greatest respect for the cloistered life and both understand and admire those who undertake the enormous challenge of a contemplative life apart from society, I no longer think it has to be the highest option.

Morality

In the travails of everyday life, one requirement for any spiritual path is often overlooked amid the techniques and goods on offer in the spiritual supermarket. In Buddhism, it is known as 'sila' or right conduct, and it is the *first* requirement and foundation for the practice of meditation, not a consequence of it. A valid argument could be made that without having first established a basis for meditation by attention to personal behaviour, such as the religious context or other structured training offers, taking up a meditation technique is premature.

Morality, like Faith, should be a work in progress. However, in the complexity of modern living, and without the guidelines of a belief-system, intelligent moment-by-moment morality is truly a heroic endeavour. The question of how to determine moral behaviour or moral issues without some precepts, some formulated guidelines to follow is one of the major challenges of our times. Not only is there no common agreement and potentially a clash of pre-set codes, but fashion and the media can be an ad-hoc arbiter of current attitudes without any deeper foundation in principle or understanding.

Glyn once said that '*morality arises from giving up authority, and love from giving up self*'. In keeping with his views on authority[3], it puts the onus on the individual to work out the basis of morality, but without a true and solid basis in principle, the result is individualistic relativism which is useless for coherence or real development. Morality based on the three Lines of Work is a good start, as the first Line means daily attention to *one's own* behavioural choices before dictating to others. No matter how well-intentioned, without an overview of the highest human potential, morality will be an ideology in some form, with all its attendant fundamental dangers.

It's a common axiom that moral corruptibility stems from the so-called root of all evil: money. Hence the wisdom of never taking payment or financial gain from any aspect of the Work

'The way to Knowledge is not for sale. It is given freely or allowed to be stolen. With any luck, someone will steal it…' In a culture where money buys everything from material goods to countless aids to happiness, health and well-being, it is an interesting position to uphold. I've had many potential meditators disappear, never to be seen again, when they realised they could not control the process with their purse. They suspected, quite rightly, that something more might be demanded of them: a personal cost in effort, commitment or change which they were not at all ready to pay.

If love arises from giving up self, the Kipling poem is also about love. That Builder gave up his ambitions and dreams to follow an inner voice, the voice from the darkness which strikes at the heart. Carving the stones was an act of love for the one who would come after.

---

1. Appendix II: Twelve Aphorisms
2. This formulation is adapted from Gurdjieff. *In Search of the Miraculous*, by PD Ouspensky
3. See discussion on authority, chapter 1

Chapter 7

Being

What is meant by the 'soul'? Prayer, meditation and contemplative experience as three aspects of developing Being and Knowledge. An evolutionary model of human growth based on the traditional eight-stage octave principle.

Not everyone who came within Glyn's orbit was comfortable with the word 'God'. I was wary myself because of the load of associations it carries, but I would often bring questions about matters of Faith, or the role of prayer or what he meant by contemplation. I would also ask about religious terms like surrender, or submission, to see what he would make of them. Early conditioning is very deep and formative, either a hindrance or strength, but is always double edged, this moulding imposed by conditions and circumstance. Conditions are never the 'truth' or the essence of anything, but it can be very hard to separate them out when something needs to change.

Once I tried to shelter from the bitterest snowstorm I have ever experienced under a stunted, bent tree on the edge of the Grand Canyon. I have a photo of a bright yellow-hooded gnome (me) huddled under its gnarled canopy amid a total white-out which had entirely deposed the glory of the canyon.

That tree was conditioned by fierce winds and adversity. In another place its essential nature may have grown into a tall magnificent specimen. But unlike the tree, as a human being I am able to know my essential nature, and with that knowledge comes freedom to choose, even in the midst of my conditioning.

This is not to say that my early religious conditioning was stunting; quite the contrary. But it did bend me in a particular direction, and something in me needed to understand before accepting any formulation as 'Truth'. Once when I went to see him on my own to explore some spiritual issue which was gnawing at me, I came up with some classical pronouncement on self-abnegation, or 'the noughting of I' derived from Christian mystical literature. Glyn looked at me quizzically:

"If it was anyone else, I'd have said 'fill yer boots'. For you—no," he said firmly.

In other words, previous conditioning, or previous understanding, is not always what is best for a person's development, though it may be fine for someone else. We all inherit concepts and ways of seeing which need to be re-visited and examined in the course of deepening and expanding our insight into deeper matters. For instance, the issue of 'no self', emptiness, unreality of the personal identity, or the multiplicity of those 'I's' we call 'me' is treated variously in different traditions, but only really has teeth when one's understanding has matured. Until that point, the words conjure up all kinds of conceptual chimera and fantasy aspirations, maybe temporarily useful, maybe a hindrance, but a wisdom teacher or Sage knows how and when to cut through them. What the 'noughting of I' would have meant to me back then I can only imagine, but it had a good ring to it.

Soul

Behind Glyn's detailed and appreciative knowledge of most religious philosophy, he was always looking to discern the fundamentals, the meaning behind customs which grow organically, or doctrines which are formulated at different times by different people, with different levels of insight. 'Soul' has many definitions. Glyn used it in general terms as '*that in you which recognises the greater.*' It is a faculty of individual psyche which has the potential to perceive and recognise more if cultured, and so become increasingly a '*crystallization of experience of the Divine.*' It should be one of the functions of religion and meditation to train us in how to accept and develop these perceptions and experience as a seed for cultivating. '*Grace*', he said, '*is an accidental perception of the Divine working.*'

However, all experience is partial by nature, conditioned, and human experience of the Divine, however overwhelming and transcendent, is also inevitably very fragmentary and conditioned by circumstances and personal factors, but it can be a seed for soul to form and grow around. Gradually, what we might call 'Soul' coheres, but, in Glyn's words, '*to the extent you assign names and labels to this type of experience, your perception of God will cohere round that seed— in ego.*'

I heard Glyn repeat versions of this point many times, but it's not an easy one to grasp: that soul can cohere in *ego*. There is a natural tendency to grab at any transcendental experience, render it clear and understandable by framing it in the language and images we are already familiar with, and then seek to communicate it to others as The Truth. It may have been very significant and formative experience, but is still a fractional product of perception, and certainly not God. Work in progress is the best attitude to soul-formation; *there is always further to go.* In the words of a Saros aphorism: *Seek the singer, not the song. The singer remains when the song has gone.*[1]

In old Zen stories, when a student brings his great experience to the Master for verification, the Master might listen, then abruptly dismiss the student or slap the table (or student) with his fan. He is offering a lesson in Emptiness, demonstrating that all forms must be left behind, and *the soul will recognise and grow from it.* Glyn might look at you intently, and move the subject on in some way, probably linking it with theory so you had a sense that it belonged somewhere in the great scheme of things, but you couldn't quite pin down where. Clearly, you could see, there was a lot further to go…

Prayer, Meditation and Contemplation

Prayer, Meditation and Contemplation are on the same spectrum and given various definitions, either seen as alternative modes of inner communion, or as sequential stages of development in the life of the soul.

Prayer turns the attention to the Divine, usually personified, and is beneficial for the turning alone; for the focus, greater perspective and uplift which is generated through genuine selfless prayer. Whether petitionary, conversational, ritualised, perfunctory or intense in nature, praying creates a field, establishing a relationship between an individual and an 'other' pole of experience outside the personal. Anecdotally, and apparently through certain controlled experiments, it is a field which can be very powerful, even to the extent of effecting material manifestations like healing. How achieved, is another question.

When the words drop out of prayer, and all that is left is

the lifting of the heart and steady attention, it becomes like *Meditation*—defined as consciousness resting in itself. Many types of continuous and chanted prayer lend themselves to this transmutation into a meditative process. Meditation itself takes many different forms, and I have described the meditation practice we followed in Chapter 4. But Glyn also said in conversation that '*all meditation is aimed at Knowledge of the Divine*'; different forms and traditions just have different ways of naming that aim. He insisted that the process of meditation is distinct from the process of daily life, but also that the ordinary senses must be functioning, so any idea that meditation takes you into a trance where you are switched off and zoned out is not describing meditation, but something else.

He added: '*Everything in the Universe is making a statement of I Am. When in meditation, seek that statement. When not in meditation, seek it externally; see it being said all around.*'

If prayer aims to put you in contact with the Divine, and meditation is a systematic means of strengthening and steadying the contact, *Contemplation* could be the experience of being in communion with It. In normal usage contemplation implies considering or thinking about something, and there is a form of thinking-non-thinking or pondering in such a way that it is like a communion with an essence. Contemplation, differentiated from prayer or meditation, is a potent formless awareness (perhaps equivalent to formless 'jhanas' in Buddhist meditation): simply 'gazing'.

However, 'gazing' (like every action) implies three things: a gazer, that which is gazed upon, and also a relationship between them—a return gazing. Without word or image, and an active not passive state, advanced contemplation may be a dissolution of the soul into the Void of darkness, or the Light of energy and love, or an inner Communion with divinity, reflecting the three personal motivations which I will describe later in this chapter. It may also be beyond all three.

'What contemplates?

Never accept any answer. That which contemplates is not the 'I', but the 'I' asks the question.

Is it the essence of your Oneness, or is it of the Nothingness from which you come?'

Contemplation is *'speculative experience of the Unconditioned... piercing the cloud of motivation.'*

'Contemplation is beauty in an instant, and breath stops.'

I think in the years leading up to his death his contemplative state is why it became harder and harder to 'find' Glyn when you engaged him in conversation. I think his gaze was directed more and more into some immensity which he would catch and render into words or diagram, in his words, *'on the way out'*. Talking about meditative experience or metaphysical issues with him in these years induced a kind of vertigo in me: I couldn't discern familiar 'mystical' landmarks and my own boundaries dissolved into the unconditioned space he inhabited. They soon came back for me, but the experience left its traces in the soul.

Metaphysical maps

The soul can develop along two lines which need to be cultivated in tandem: a *Line of Knowledge/Mind* and a *Line of Being*. If one line is favoured and the other neglected, it results in a 'stupid saint' (over-emphasis on Being), or a theoretical meta-physicist with all the 'answers' but little transformative experience for a genuine foundation (over-dependence on Mind).

Glyn's appointed task, with the help of all those he drew into his orbit over many years, was to offer a revised metaphysical map to supplement those currently available from religious and esoteric traditions. Revised, not so much in content, as in language and presentation. The problem with older maps is that the language and location do not chime with the Mind of today, so the academic study of interpreting, comparing, inter-relating etc. tends to provide a diversion from the meaning content. All too often scholarly teaching creates a forest of concepts, and Being slips away between the trees. We certainly need maps, but the best maps speak directly from Being, which is not so common, and even those are modified through the centuries as many minds enjoy themselves with detail and intricacies, rather than penetrating to the core. The core is Being. Contemporary maps with such power are very rare.

From Glyn's work, the model I found easiest to work with was a basic developmental model of human psychology which we called *The Double Diamond* because of its diamond-shaped layout. At the end of this chapter I will present a very succinct summary of the basic principles of it.

I used the Double Diamond, (alternatively called the Human Octave), as the focus of a group in my home. Following the pattern outlined in my previous chapter, for several years on Tuesday night I would leave my front door on the latch. As eight o'clock approached, people would start to slip in and sit in the front room, which I had prepared through physical arrangement and metaphysical intent to make it into a common space, temporarily not my private room. Some people arrived a bit early for a meditation check. At eight o'clock, the door was closed and three candles lit. We meditated for about twenty minutes, then discussed some aspect of the theory, reporting back on observations and exercises undertaken during the week.

Glyn's insight expressed itself in diagrams. They are not as pretty as Tibetan mandalas, but serve a similar function: powerful, detailed representations of living forces, expressed as abstract principles or symbols. He encapsulated his teaching best in geometry, or in gnomic verbal descriptions which contain but don't explain the system. Unlocking the significance requires study to turn it into wisdom.

Mandalas, beautiful detailed circular and symmetric diagrams are valued for their artistry and beauty, but leaving aside merely decorative modern patterns, traditional mandalas fuse geometric and symbolic teachings into a condensed picture of the universe. However, the potential for internal embodiment as lived teachings will only open up from years of study and contemplation. Meditating or contemplating a mandala helps to integrate the deeper knowledge of the tradition visually depicted in it, so to make it meaningful you need to be grounded in something of that knowledge and background. Likewise, Glyn's diagrams are study-tools, focus for discussion, and he saw them as compendiums for preserving esoteric teaching into the future.

Glyn gave away his ideas and time freely, and declined any gifts. Many years ago, as the online revolution gathered pace, a number of people clubbed together and bought him a computer, feeling that he could make good use of it. Buying it without asking him first was designed to be a fait accompli and a ruse to short-circuit any of the expected objections. Even then he refused to take it. After some negotiation, he hit on a solution: we could give it to his son. So, we did, and over the years his family became expert at rendering and animating theory at his direction, but he himself stuck to scrap paper or large out-of-date yearbooks, picked up for a song at the market. And in these, freehand and with meticulously neat detail, he drew out his 'mandalas'.

Summary of the Double Diamond as a model for Growth

The model describes the potential development span of an individual in simple terms, through recognisable stages/ functions which are derived from esoteric philosophy not modern psychological or psychoanalytical theory.

Musicians are familiar with the musical octave, an ordering of vibrational frequencies into whole tones and two half-tones called intervals. Esoteric philosophy claims this pattern is taken from a more ancient wisdom, which recognised the same process as a natural Law of universal dynamics. It consisted of eight steps with two half-steps or change points. Of particular importance is the role of these two intervals where the 'vibrations' are less, because the unfolding process, whatever it is, may either come to a halt or diverge because of diminished energy at these points.

All the energy transactions which sustain a living cosmos (each of us is an individual cosmos, enmeshed in other cosmoses) operate this way: smaller octaves filling the interval points in larger octaves to provide the extra boost of energy needed to continue in the same chosen direction. Without some boost of extra energy input at these interval points, the whole process diverts slightly, leading to a change of overall direction which is often not noticed in human affairs. Or it stops altogether and never reaches completion. Many grand plans falter either at the first or second interval. The energy boosts can be a shock, or a new octave beginning.[2] It seems complex, but nature is complex, and this patterning of process is observable and experiential.

Cosmologically, the Human Octave begins at an interval point in a greater Octave of all Creation, whose boundless purpose is beyond our ken. The specific purpose of human being within this vast program of conscious evolution is *to supply the necessary consciousness for this interval, so that our energy and awareness will enable the process of creation to unfold its purpose.* As a rationale for human existence, this concept works as well as any and better than most!

The Human Octave

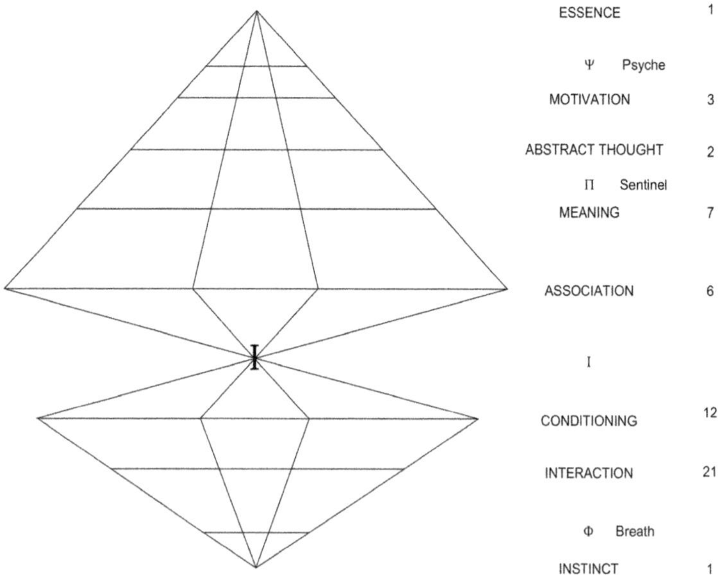

The all-important focus of the organising principle of Self ('I'), is situated near the centre joining the upper and lower diamonds, which are not equal sizes. The upper being larger than the lower is perhaps a visual representation of the 'extent' of the Unknown in our make-up. The entire octave represents the fullest development of individual human being from our common core as a species in Instinct, to the Essence which we all share by virtue of being human. The labels are as neutral and precise as possible, stripped of fanciful associations or mythological resonance.

You will see four intervals rather than two in the diagram. *Breath, I, Sentinel and Psyche* are points where conscious change can occur. The Sentinel and Breath are effective intervals for the *involutionary process*, the 'down-flowing' of cosmic or creative force from the origin of consciousness, while 'I' and Psyche are significant intervals in the *evolutionary* thrust of striving for greater consciousness. My summary here is based on an evolutionary growth pattern (upward flow). The numbers beside the names, 1, 21, 12, 6, 7, 2, 3, 1 are symbolic, and too much to explain in a short synopsis.

Instinct (1)

Well below our conscious threshold are all the instinctive urges which propel the survival and life of the species. In the interests of the species, instinctive programming at a biological and psychological level is buried too deep for easy conscious manipulation, but it can be damaged, and is also a source of power, which certain yogic, shamanic or meditative practices can tap.

Breath (interval)

The first breath after emergence from the womb is the first interaction with the external environment. Breath changes body chemistry, and is utilised by many meditative methods. Different breath patterns reflect different states of the organism. One of the rules of discipline is 'Remember the breath at all times.'

Interaction (21)

On the journey of life, everything is interaction: with others, the senses and environment, light, colour, sound, body sensations, people's responses. Through this omnipresent network of interactions, the psyche is gradually conditioned into particular patterns by the specifics of the environment.

Conditioning (12)

Personal identity is created through the interaction of both external circumstances and the internal conditioning of innate tendencies and instinct. By about the age of seven, these multitudinous interactions and conditioning naturally cohere into a distinct sense of self or 'I'. Conditioning is necessary and unavoidable, but also a constraint. It binds behaviour and attitudes into patterns, some of which should be outgrown, or were negative to start with. With conscious work, they can be replaced by healthier patterns. The conditioned self ('I') is not the same as one's individual nature (Psyche).

The zodiac is divided into twelve, like the months of the year, and astrologically the twelve represent a complete range of identities. Only twelve patterns result if you connect up six points in a continuous line. These we called 'sigils' and one is at the beginning of each chapter of this book.[3]

'I' – self (interval)

This is the command-centre of individual Being we call 'I', or me/myself/ego, organizing the many identities which make up our personality, and putting order on our experience. Yet there is more to experience than 'I' normally encompasses. In Glyn's words: *'The depth of an experience is not 'I', but 'I' keys it in and remembers it.'*

Association (6)

This is about the normal thinking process, which involves making associations and connections between ideas, experience, memory. It is quite automatic in ordinary mentation; one thought or idea leading to another and connected all together into conclusions and ideas. A good thinker is a good organiser, insightfully associating categories into new arrangements. Meditators, however, wish the mind's associating-process would take a rest, so seemingly resistant is it to efforts to control it at will.

Meaning (7)

Making life meaningful, whether through a job, hobby, interest, family concerns, sport, sexual drive, religion, spirituality etc. is an emotional drive, without which depression and suffering can take hold of the emotions. Meaningfulness is emotion with a direction.

Everything described so far feeds into the sense of self and personality at 'I' between the upper and lower sections. Only when there is interest and intent to reach beyond 'I', beyond what is normally meaningful, is further exploration and growth possible, but there is an interval to be overcome.

Sentinel (interval)

The amygdala is called the 'emotional sentinel' of the brain, and in this model, there is a natural protective mechanism which arrests or permits further growth. The personality and sense of 'I' is generally protected from forces which could disturb or threaten its integrity or balance, including higher order influences which could be too challenging to the status quo of current wellbeing.

However, an alert internal sentinel can sense what is valuable. Mine was instantly alerted at the first meeting with Glyn. I knew he represented something important, and I was ready to take it on. The same function caused others to take flight immediately on meeting him. Whether they put it down to aversion to the smoke-haze, alarm at being seen through, or something else, they were not psychologically ready or willing for this journey, and the sentinel in them was doing its job.

Meditation trains and refines sentinel, allowing the embrace of new realities, new powers, new horizons with safety. Providing the interval is filled with fresh impetus, from here on upwards the octave unfolds and becomes more accessible, usually through special conditions.

True/Abstract Thought (2)

Unlike ordinary associative thinking, this kind of thought is engaged by contemplation of abstract ideas and images, or can operate without image. It is creative, as when problems mulled over at length suddenly resolve, or issues gestating quietly in the back of the mind emerge fruitfully formed. It is as if some great internal wheel has been turning, in silence.

Motivations (3)

Deep emotional biases shape our Being, for the most part unrecognised. Some of us intuitively see reality in terms of *Light*, and manifest an unconscious attraction towards clarity, display, ordering and beauty. Motivated by *Dark,* a person is drawn to the profound creative darkness of the origins of things, and wants to *know.* A *Communion* motivation predisposes people towards relationship, unifying and bringing things together. Through these three lenses, human beings perceive God and the Divine quest, shaped by their template of natural bias, and the predilections are reflected in the communities into which people gather.

So deep and generally unconscious are these primal motivations, that whichever lens your own nature is predisposed to view reality through, (usually one is predominant) will be Truth for you, *the* Truth, and other views are partial, mistaken, erroneous. It is extremely difficult to overcome the bias of one's own motivation, but it is possible.

To recognise and respect the deep essential motivational drive in others *which we do not share because of the force of our own* is an achievement of some magnitude in the personal sphere and would have virtually miraculous consequences for social collaboration. Glyn maintained that the motivations are not subject to reason but can be subject to the right kind of observation. Ultimately, we must learn to see beyond the colouration of our own and learn to see and respect all motivations, finally knowing there is further to go beyond any colouration.

Psyche (interval)

In this model Psyche equates to the *totality* of an individual's psychology, which will include personality characteristics but is much more primary and total, an expression of 'true nature' individualised, with powers which mostly remain unconscious or inaccessible.

Essence (1)

Essence and Instinct are shared hallmarks of the human species. Like a distillation, our Essence is our humanity as opposed to a different animal or another species. From the human perspective, Essence is perceived as 'God', an expression of Spirit, or more precisely, 'God in you'. Essence and Instinct are One.

To sum up, this entire Human Octave fills the gap in the greater cosmic Octave of Creation. Our awareness is our contribution to the evolution of the Cosmos.

---

1. Aphorisms. See Appendix II.
2. See *In Search of the Miraculous* by PD Ouspensky for a detailed summary of how the principles of Octave theory were presented in the system of Gurdjieff, a different mythology and elaboration from the Saros Double Diamond, but the principles of octave and intervals are explained in some detail.
3. See Appendix 1.

Chapter 8

Play

Ritual training. In Hindu mythology all creation is seen as play, 'lila', the joyful, spontaneous interaction between the Absolute and the empirical world of its creation. We took our play seriously too.

Every traditional culture has a sacred creation myth, a narrative of how the world and creatures came into being, and which explains the process of world creation—except for the very beginning, which can't be 'explained'. The point of origin is a mystery in every version, simply because it *is* a mystery, though various elucidations are attempted for it in different mythic accounts, and the scientific myth has its own story. We need to discard the materialist idea that creation myths are a primitivist attempt at *history*, and understand that the context and intent is mythic: a metaphysical explanatory model of creative process which can be as relevant in your life now as in the time or culture of its origin. It may need a little disentangling and interpreting however, to bring out its contemporary relevance.

The creation narrative we worked with was a metaphysical structure which on occasions we acted out to embed the principles in body, mind and perception. Like the rest of my account in this book, I shall present the barest outline so as not to overwhelm the narrative in obscure theorizing which needs a different route of approach.

Our sequence begins, like many others, with the conception of Unity, because there really is no other starting point. From Unity, *one* individual point arises (how or why are the bigger questions!). It is a point of origin with potential to develop further into multiplicity. This One instantaneously as it were, (time is not yet existent) becomes Three, as the originating creative impulse ricochets from *one into three.*

The logic here accords with the universal principle of Triplicity, three in one. It is not division into duality because of 'action and response': the *impulse* triggers response, which is in effect a *denial* of it and precipitates a move to *return* to the pre-action state. Hence three actions take place—the original, the response, and the outcome or unification. Only then can time and space (expressions of the duality of our consciousness) be established and creation continue to unfold.

Many well-known cosmologies represent triplicity, the first level of manifestation, by a Trinity of gods, or aspects of the one God, or Jewels of the tradition, pillars of the Tree and so on. The dynamic is always the same: a Will (affirming/active), a response (denying/passive) and an outcome or balancing (unifying/equilibrating), but the sequence itself is dynamic and the roles the three forces play vary depending on whether they are beginning, middle or end. The whole dynamic establishes the complexity of creation. Every time you pick up a cup, every social interaction, every project undertaken is a dance of Three. A triangle is a dynamic symbol as compared with a circle or square.

From the Book of Jubilee, a primer of Saros philosophy, I quote :

> *All that has existence is contained by* ***Unity****. Unity is within all that exists. Will is the* ***One****, the Father of Creation. She that maintains the Integrity of Unity, She is the Mother of Creation. Her* ***three*** *aspects rest within Unity until called forth by the Father's action.*
>
> *The activity of Will in the Mother creates the* ***Gate*** *of Necessity: on one side potential, on the other potency. These* ***twin*** *poles set in their place the* ***seven*** *pillars of creation, the Potencies which frame the temple of the* ***six*** *Constructors who set their hands to the task of world creation. These artisans work in pairs, in triples, in fours and in sixes to make and build the four levels of creation.…all they that depend upon that one artisan are* ***twelve****. Twelve, twelve, twelve, they combine in* ***twenty-one*** *governances …*[1]

On different occasions we danced this sequence, we presented it whilst Turning (as in the whirling meditation), we made a drama of it. On one occasion I was Affirming Mother, gyrating round a brave man trying to stand his ground as the One first principle, while I and two other women (Denying and Unifying Mothers) did our best to weave circles round him. Dance and movement can render abstract ideas into visible, three-dimensional forms, and embed them in body cells, not just brain cells as ideas, which is also the function and intent of all religious and ceremonial ritual. If it is conducted with dignity and symbolic flair, ritual will engage all parts of the organism, body, emotions and intellect, making it a living experience, and informing the psyche.

Rules of ritual

Glyn seemed to be a master at ritual and ceremony, speaking the language of ritual like a native. Undoubtedly, he had been trained himself, and though he would never talk about his background, it was an era when old magical traditions were being revitalised. Either that or he had picked it up through his extensive reading in the British Library where he had a reading card. However, he was determined to rid the genre of dramatics with special garments and ringing invocations prefaced by "Oh Great XX, vouchsafe thy xxx" and the like. The predominant power of this kind of ritual performed for dramatic effect is generally to enhance the status and self-belief of the performers, its psycho-logic tuned to personal ends rather than strengthening collective values. Glyn had studied the great rituals of English public life, the Queen's coronation, the Opening of Parliament and Black Rod, for example, and noted the effect as well as being moved by the manner of their conduct and the seriousness of the intent behind them. These rituals are effective; they work to seal a change, to establish and cohere, to signal a different state or status, which happens by effecting the consciousness of all who take part or witness.

The power of effective religious ritual to shift consciousness depends on the same principles, but archaic or elaborate costume is not intrinsic to the power, and not actually needed if the psychological intent is clear. The combination of a clear intention and consciously performed gesture can summon up the kind of potency which is able to move more than merely emotions. Effective ritual is non-personal. We were instructed in maintaining a 'matter-of-fact approach', formal enough to set the parameters for establishing a non-personal space, but not stiff or pompous, which is what happens if self-importance gets into the act.

The roles common in esoteric and sacred ritual also set these parameters. For example, it is useful to appoint someone to act as a formal 'Door-keeper', obliging anyone wishing to enter the space to knock, wait, and present themselves for perusal before being permitted entry. For any conscious and ritual work, scattered attention and self-involvement are impediments, so the pause and slight tension created by having to pass a Door-keeper concentrates attention into the moment. The person who then enters the ritual context is not the person who was recently rushing round Tesco, or the frustrated driver hunting for a parking space ten minutes before. Unless of course, for a highly 'evolved' person, their daily rituals of shopping and parking took place with that same quality of awareness and inner space!

Glyn loved ritual, and appreciated how profoundly it could move the soul. Ritual is capable of facilitating a greater shift in two minutes than two hours of discourse. He ran a course back in the 80's which set the basic training in place.

A typical training on that course was to hold a state or implement steadily for a long period. For example, to embody the Law of Three Forces[2], three people stood in a row holding a symbol and an inward identification with active, passive or equilibrating, and did not move for exactly half an hour. Then all changed places, and stood for another half hour, and changed again half an hour later. By then all had held the active affirming force for half an hour, then the passive denying for another half hour, then the neutral or unifying force, all the while standing motionless, holding inwardly and outwardly. This pattern was repeated throughout one whole day, so that each person had covered all six variants of the possible orders in which three forces could express.

Boring? It certainly was, but it developed will and an uncommon sense of purpose and achievement in holding attention against its natural wandering grain for such long periods, and became a standard training for certain ritual work. Exercises like this trained steadiness of mind, will, and detachment, and not so much sorted the sheep from the goats, as made certain they were on an equal footing and had conquered restlessness and the bug of boredom.

We also learned how to create a working space by sealing the corners in different ways. Sealing means using people or symbolic objects to mark each point delineating the space of the room, symbolically sealing it from outside influences, and concentrating its field. Once a room was prepared this way with the corners established, the whole atmosphere changed, a psychological phenomenon mainly, but perhaps space itself can hold charge or memory. Once the work is over, the room is unsealed, by sequencing the actions in reverse and scattering the field created. '*Ritual is an exercise in psycho-logic*'. The symbolic actions and implements must make sense, and resonate correctly and effectively with the aim they are intended to activate.

What sort of aims are consonant with a path of Knowledge? Nothing material (trying to manipulate circumstances in the world) and nothing personal. The point of ritual training is the *training*, which means developing the discernment to recognise the factors which in daily life can set atmospheres, create situations and change states of awareness. Every day in home, office, and commercial premises spaces are being set for particular purposes, our psyches and reactions are being manipulated by gestures, (a wave, an approach with folded arms, two fingers) actions with symbolic purpose (removing a wedding-ring), arrangements of furniture or objects (flowers on a desk, chairs arranged in a circle). My very young son once knew how to change his little sister's state with the raise of an eyebrow. That was all it took to set her off, and her peace of mind (and ours) was instantly disrupted. Clearly there was history behind that symbolic gesture, and he used it with devilish effect!

At the beginning of this ritual training course, the Long Room of the centre we rented at that time was carefully cleared, swept and dusted with attention. A bowl of water and towel was placed outside the door to wash before entering, with obvious symbolism, and designed to collect the attention and bring a person into the present moment. By the end of the course that room was positively humming. Therefore, at the end the room needed to be unsealed and the energies dissipated, as its working purpose was fulfilled. After reversing the sealing process, nothing dissipates an energetic charge quicker than random chaotic noise and movement. Order builds; chaos dissipates.

Ritual can speak to more than just the head or intellect, or emotion. Emotion is easily stirred through beauty or art, and religious and ceremonial ritual. However, the power to change state, to teach through action and express through gesture, to elevate beyond emotion into the still space which touches on other worlds, this was new experience to me. I was familiar with Church ritual and appreciated its resonance when conducted with dignity and a bit of pomp and splendour, but Glyn's approach was something else. Simple, with a minimum of cues and absolute attention to detail, psycho-logic was engaged with precision, and demanded that you keep your attention always outward on the language of symbol and gesture, not on your thoughts and emotions or even intention, all of which bring yourself into the picture. The logic of the action carries the intention. Inside you can be silent.

From the discipline of mental and emotional training, the reward after intensive work was to know states of energy so fine and high and beyond the personal that the body thrummed, the mind was clear and silent, and the heart was open, clean and utterly responsive to any breeze from the Unknown Regions. One could hear the rustle of angel wings before the Throne; the susurration of heavenly hosts massing in the corners, the tinkle of crystal pavements in the courts of the King.

It was enthralling, but not always easy. In one long complex ritual I had been standing for a very long time at one end of the room holding a crown symbolising the One at the base of the Creation Octave. There was a lot going on and much of it must have been channelled down to this point because I began to feel decidedly queer, with energies circulating through my head and threatening to cause a blackout. "Must hold on. Mustn't drop it" I was saying to myself through gritted teeth, as the thought of disrupting the entire scene and hurling the crown to the ground was too awful to contemplate. But I could not sustain it. The next thing I heard was a tiny wavering voice, mine, cutting through the solemn proceedings: "Glyn. I can't hold it any longer…"

"Aid her!" roared Glyn from the other end of the room. Two women leaped to my side, took the crown, and I promptly fainted, and was half-carried from the room.

Someone took my place and the ritual carried on. Afterwards Glyn used it for a lesson on succour and aid, which I missed as I was being aided and succoured. My mistake, he explained to me later, was to try to block what I felt arising and hang on to my normal awareness. If I had let the energy through, it would have precipitated a powerful change of state.

He must have enjoyed putting this course together, and thinking about it now, I suspect he poured into it all he had learned. We provided him with the people and the opportunity to put his expertise and love of symbol in action into practice, a rare thing. We were unspoiled by other training or allegiances, we accepted discipline and we worked. We worked damn hard on our personal peccadillos on courses like this, to overcome resistances from the ego, to bear with other people—for the sake of the Work. Always the sense that we worked together for Knowledge, and to be able to perpetuate it.

Glyn also designed another intensive course of great beauty and power which was run several times over the years by different people, and brought forth the intrinsic qualities of the numbers 3, 4, 5 and 6 and their effect on the psyche. To detail this course would be a spoiler, and meaningless, since again, it spoke without words. No one who experienced that course ever forgot it, or what it opened up of what some might call 'the heavenly regions', the unknown powers and reaches in one's own psyche. Numbers were never the same again either.

Resources

The demands of this kind of work created the conditions for much laughter and witticism. In our late-night sessions, we would gather together in a motley collection of old arm-chairs and sofas, festooned with ash-trays, and go over the events of the day. Glyn was always the centre, always finding ways to teach, always the butt of irreverent joshing if someone could make it witty enough. The 'Welsh Wizard' rolled his tobacco and threw out challenges to generate argument, eyeing us under his brows through a curling plume of smoke. As people drifted off to bed, a hard core always remained into the wee small hours. I couldn't always make it. After greedily propping open my eyes as long as possible, sometimes I reluctantly crawled off to bed, wondering what I might miss, and consoling myself that it would probably go very theoretical and abstract if only the cerebral types remained!

It was always an early start in the morning. Some people didn't seem to need sleep, and indeed, when the energy level is high enough, a couple of hours will do.

Ever resourceful, if we needed some item as a symbolic object in a ritual, we either made it, or improvised. In general, Glyn was insistent that for an instrument to have any power, it had to be made from scratch, with all the concentrated attention and sweat of the maker imbuing it with conscious intent. That logic actually works. For the non-crafty, like myself, it was a challenge, but I have made several, including beating metal into the shape of a breast-plate and engraving it. A breastplate protects the heart. On courses, we had to improvise, so the kitchen was regularly raided. Glyn once walked into a concentrated ritual situation wearing a black plastic bag. Far from laughter, the atmosphere galvanised instantly with the power his presence generated, and the bag could have been a black silken robe sprinkled with live stars. It hardly needed him to stamp his staff to send a quiver up the spine.

Using a few items is useful to convey intention, to speak the language of meaning. For example, receptivity is traditionally associated with a cup or bowl with obvious reference. To choose one, as well as the basic shape, you have to weigh up the qualities particular to each and decide if it will create the right resonance and help establish the correct field for the purpose. Size, weight, colour etc are like words in the condensed ritual sentence being spoken by, and to, the whole field of the psyche. There's also a lovely process of serendipity: 'Ah. That's just right', even though it might be unexpected and not what you first thought of. The mechanism for this process is light, open attention, using the back of the head and the heart, and in this way, too, sentimentality is avoided. The sentimental is often described as 'syrupy' and the metaphor is apt; it feels like syrup or too much sugar, and you feel it in the front of chest and brain.

Admittedly, the black plastic bag obeyed none of these rules. Its lesson was: use anything or nothing—it's the field that counts. As a practical training in simplicity, we had what became known as the Kitchen-Sink Ritual, in which the room was filled with an assortment of heterogeneous objects, and the participants had to decide which would be useful for ritual purposes. Gradually, everything was thrown out again.

Following the tradition of making and empowering symbolic objects (by attention), we all turned our hand to practical crafts at certain points. I was often astonished at the skill with which things were produced, and glad of the opportunity it provided to work with the hands—part of the ethos of an all-round education of thought, emotion and action. A fabulous large gong of heavy solid brass with a glyph carved out of the middle which rang at just a particular pitch to sound the beginning and end of sessions was one such wonder. Many people had a hand in it, talented craftspeople able to work with metal and wood, but the design was Glyn's inspiration. Making items is grounding, frustrating sometimes, but a training in attentiveness and patience, and a corrective to the hegemony of the intellect, or emotional indulgence.

As for gesture, a story was told of how Glyn once raised an arm and wiggled his fingers in the air in the course of a ritual, using the gesture like an antenna to find or channel power. Sometime later a young man was seen in a different context performing the same gesture. Glyn pounced, "What are you doing?"

The young man was startled. "There's been a bat flying around. As kids this was how we summoned bats," he said innocently.

Power

Given our emphasis on self-responsibility and independent thinking, and with exposure to other levels of reality, there was always a danger of developing arrogance and an attraction to power. Glyn had ways of curbing this tendency, and the group dynamics themselves did a good job of cutting down to size, but ritual work involves handling power, so it is especially important to put counters in place.

One memorable occasion on a course, probably judging we were getting a bit big for our boots, he quietly established a chair at the top of some stairs, and set someone upon it. Then, choosing a time when most people were absorbed in some casual and enjoyable exercise, Glyn appeared in the room and silently beckoned people out one by one. Outside the door, he indicated the person on the chair and announced to each newcomer: "There is your King who holds your life in his hands". He pointed to the floor: "On your knees and crawl to your King!" he commanded.

Startled, most took the challenge, and crawled on hands and knees along the hall and up the stairs in humility and homage to whoever had been established as the King. A couple of people balked, but went along with it, except that their demeanour and attitude revealed something less than humility. "More like the prowling of a lion than a subject approaching his master" Glyn commented later to general merriment, and the offenders had been made to crawl all the way back again, while everybody else had returned on foot.

It was play-acting with a purpose, because lessons learned from observing your own responses when faced with this kind of challenge to ego and self-image are rarely forgotten. However, respect for other's choices as self-responsible beings is an essential ingredient. There is no knowledge value in controlling others, and very real dangers on both sides. In our approach no one was ever forced into anything, and in fact, those who had problems conforming to instructions provided the liveliest and most valuable feedback when they contributed an honest account to the general review sessions at the end of each day. The evening reviews were integral to the work. They were cathartic for everyone, enormously entertaining, and often moving. They served as release of tension, feedback mechanism, and an opportunity to assimilate one's own experience as well as learn from others. It is the nature of subtle experience to vanish from recollection unless it is teased forth by reflection, and stored in consciousness.

The great Octave of Creation[3] with which I started this chapter is myth. It is also a working model, a way of breaking down the seamless and cyclical garment of creation into a sequence, analysing and establishing natural universal principles based in number and the symbolic resonance of numbers in the continuity of our experience. It doesn't get much simpler than the symbolism of number, and develops a capacity to be 'at home' in a more abstract mind, exercising faculties which are increasingly relevant not just for inner work but for the general direction in which humanity is heading in a digital, quantum age.

For a slightly different 'take' on the mystery of creation, I was amused to find recently among my notes a little poem I had created, on a page otherwise filled with analysis of powerful imagery from Genesis and references to 'flaming swords'. It read:

How odd of God
To take a clod
And make a man
Of little span,
Then set a Tree
To torment he
And send him out.

Without a doubt
All that forgetting
And much begetting
Is quite a change
And very strange,
Extremely odd of God!

Clearly, I had suffered from too much exaltation!

Even without actions, the effect of walking into a room lovingly and precisely laid out to abstract principles can create silence in a breath.

I see a great blue glass bowl on a snow-white cloth, six shining bowls around it,
twelve smaller in polished brass surrounding.
Three candles precisely spaced, burning behind.
In the shadowy corners of the room, earth, air, fire and water, the elements of our incarnation.

And we can pause in such a space, surrounded by tangible poetry, and let the heart rise up, as once expressed in the greatest love-song of any sacred encounter:

> "Rise up, my love, my fair one, and come away. For lo, the winter is past, the rain is over and gone. The flowers appear on the earth, the time of the singing of birds has come, and the voice of the turtledove is heard in our land."[4]

---

1. The Book of Jubilee, Cranswick Press 1984
2. Sometimes known as: affirming, denying, & neutralising/harmonising
3. Appendix I for diagram
4. Song of Solomon 2.11

Chapter 9

Temples

'The Lord is in his Holy Temple; let all the world keep silence before him'
Sacred space and Temple symbolism, and the inner Temple. War, suffering and sacrifice, and a look to the future.

I am standing below the earth heaped above me these many thousand years in a Neolithic mound. Before me a narrow passage to the sunlight, and behind me, an enormous rock shields a small chamber. I enter the chamber and, in the darkness, six thousand years of silence wraps round me. 'This was no place for bones', I thought. 'This was where man and woman could come to hear the pulse of the earth and be lifted beyond themselves and their daily concerns of food, shelter and social life.' If I could hear it, they could hear it. The way down can be a way up, like a wormhole in space, and our forebears seemed to have a penchant for taking this route.

Then again, deep, deep in the earth below the Dordogne in France, on rocky ledges of extraordinary awkwardness, far from any source of light, delicate bison and other animals drawn with utmost tenderness have been cavorting for forty thousand years. The guide's voice was hushed, hesitant, as if afraid to pierce with his words the veil of a time and place, so long ago it seemed like another universe. It seemed like that to me; as if my modern brain and psyche was ill-equipped to make contact with the consciousness of beings like me, but yet not like me. Other.

And once I stood on a hill above Delphi. The crowds had gone and evening was descending. White birds circled above the ruins, and I looked down the natural bowl of the valleys, blue rimmed on blue, fading away to the distant sea. 'What a place for a temple! They really knew how to awaken the oracle', I thought, as that whole oracular sense in me began to stir. Make a magnificent space in a magnificent place and Lo, any human being with half a soul will sense the possibilities hidden behind the veil!

Humanity has created external sacred spaces, Temples, for as long as the species has existed. Natural places with special qualities like caves and grottos, became structures which were purposely built on specific sites. Some of earth's sacred places are no more than a small circle of stones, others are gigantic feats of primitive engineering, while the evolution of cultures and technologies developed towering structures of almost unbelievable ornateness, as in the elaborate temples of India, the massive carvings on temples in Cambodia like Angkor Watt, and the elegant traceries of stone and glass of Europe's great gothic cathedrals.

How much effect do surroundings have? What power might be inherent in the structure itself, for instance as a simple example, a building on a four-square base as opposed to a building on a six-sided base? Would there be a difference in the quality or presence of the space created from the different geometries? Does the type of structure have an effect on the imagination, and how would this be relevant to the sacred?

It's not at all controversial to recognise that the characteristics of a surrounding space have psychological effect. Awkward or chaotic surroundings can make you feel uncomfortable, while in others it is easy to relax, or feel inspired and energised. It is also observable that designated spaces repeatedly used for sacred purposes become 'charged' like a battery with a residue of some kind of power or energy, a magnetic field which anyone even a little 'tuned in' can feel the moment he or she enters it. The question is, what in you accords with the space, and why? It implies that the *space itself has structure and presence,* both of which arise as the product of *conscious* input, not accident. When they conform to universal principles of number and geometry, the architectural proportions palpably deliver conscious intent.

Without elaborating on these principles, which have been known and practised in all civilizations for thousands of years, my point is simply that a *Field* to which human consciousness responds can be deliberately created and preserved. However, even in the natural landscape, it is that same human consciousness responding to natural features which causes a sense of the sacred to be stirred, and then repetition or elaboration strengthens the response.

Irrespective of culture, the symbol *Temple* represents highest values. Hence, compared with dwellings for personal living, many sacred spaces are monumental in size and conception, and are the product of almost superhuman effort, and are also designed and intended to endure through time—to conquer time perhaps. Sacred experience is translated into matter. Interestingly, the word 'Temple' meaning a 'place of worship', and the temples at the sides of the head, both seem to derive from the proto-Indo-European root '*ten-*' meaning 'to stretch'. The stretching of cords and posts to mark out a space for placing stones or earth-work according to precise principles may be this origin.

Tension

Tension is the paradox at the heart of a Temple. Tension is not necessarily negative. It is produced by an interlocking of forces. Consider the tension of the structure which maintains the huge unsupported domes of the Duomo in Florence or Hagia Sophia, or the soaring arches of a gothic cathedral. Tension contributes to meditation, tensions of the body holding a posture for long periods, and tensions of mind returning and returning to a single point and holding back the free flow of thought. These are tensions in stillness, tensions of contrary forces so poised they can hold beauty steady, and generate peace. The paradox of living Peace is that it is *dynamic* not static. It's the product of forces, not of absence of force. The centre of the rope in an evenly matched tug-of-war can be perfectly still.

When 'stressed', you might like to consider how your stress could be converted to tension instead, and used more productively. There is actually no growth of consciousness without tension, so if your life is full of forces pulling in different directions, stop and take a breath. *This is where you build your Temple*, right in the midst of your life, and then its tensions can be transformed creatively. From a potent pause and stepping back, to the ongoing cultivation of an integrated life and a silent mind, we can create a space which opens to the sacred for *real*.

There is a central point, a still point, between that which is potential and everything which manifests. It's a point of choice, of conscious choice. In the Saros creation myth, it was named the Gate of Consciousness, the Gates of Life and Death, the Supreme Event or the Spindle of Necessity.

The *Spindle of Necessity,* taken from a myth in Plato's Republic, has several elements which Glyn must have found illuminating. It is said that all the circles of life revolve around the central spindle, and the spindle turns on a single point. This singularity is its root in Oneness, and the Spindle is suspended from a column of light extending through heaven and earth. The entire space (called the Afterlife in Plato), is a Temple-space, with openings above and below through which souls are ascending and descending. We will look again at this myth in the context of death and rebirth in a later chapter. It was so close to the core of Glyn's philosophy that almost the last words I heard him speak as he was dying referred to it. Only now, so many years later, am I beginning to understand those final words, and the centrality of the Temple in his life and thought.

Daily we make choices to sustain or ignore the sacredness of the mythic Temple linking above and below. We might call it a Temple of Meaning, representing all that is most meaningful to us as individuals and our deeper aspirations, but there is always this element of choice and its consequences. Through meditation, in states of heightened awareness, we *hold the tension between the poles of the pillars*, and can know the potency and emptiness which is present before the self, 'I', attaches to a thought or feeling.

"Wisdom has built her house, she has hewn out her seven pillars" (Proverbs 9:1)

The mythic Temple structure has seven pillars made of the three primal forces (affirming, denying, unifying).[1] Think of pillars as separate forces within us. Three turn into six by polarizing, which will be the subject of the next chapter, because polarity sets up a creative field just as a magnetic field is created from two poles dynamically separated. In this Temple field, a spontaneous creative influx comes into being, like a seventh pillar in the centre. It is a point of contact with the divine world of origin and potential, but veiled from us until we bring it into our awareness and enter the silent space of the internal Temple: a place of refreshment, peace, wisdom and Knowledge.

In Glyn's words:

> *"To know some-thing, you have to separate. Then you rest between the Known and the Unknown without being attached to the Known."*

The *Known* includes all those powerful, moving visions and wondrous non-ordinary experiences which for many people are the incentives to embark on a path of meditation and spiritual questing. Potent spiritual experiences are adventures in the Temple courtyard, but not necessarily entry to the Holy of Holies, according to all the profound mystical teaching of the world.

Conflict

Tension and polarization aren't necessarily the same as *conflict.* Contrary to its generally negative and stressful connotations, Glyn was very pro-conflict as an important mechanism for generating energy (and consequently, awareness) and he was no slouch at its creation himself! One had to be alert around him, for Ego thrives on conflict, always willing to think the worst, take offence or elevate self above others. It's a rarely observed contradiction that those who subscribe to easy platitudes about 'peace and love' actually make themselves more vulnerable to conflictual forces outside their control. True peace and love are a result of mature understanding and working with situations of conflict, both external and internal.

Conflict plainly arises in life everywhere, at all levels. Less obvious is the idea that the outcome of conflict situations can resolve in any of three ways: *destructive, futile, or creative.* It is the way human conflict is handled which determines which of the three it becomes, so let's take a closer look.

The easiest to identify and which probably gives conflict its normal bad press, is *destructive conflict,* in which one 'force' simply overpowers and destroys the other. End of conflict and new situation.

Of longer duration, and potentially even more destructive to well-being, is *futile conflict.* It counts as futile when a conflicting situation has been sustained long past its usefulness with no outcome either positive or negative. The parties engaged in a futile conflict sustain it because they do not recognise its futility, and are determined to keep it going, assuming that at any moment they personally will prevail. Many arguments in a relationship take on this character.

The craziest aspect of this sort of futile conflict, by definition only visible to those outside it, is that it absorbs all the energy of the conflicting parties into maintaining itself. Hence the conflict itself grows stronger (or the lawyers!), while the protagonists are generally weakened by it. When conflict is so self-sustaining (think of long-running feuds), it is hard to resolve or shift the ground without either accident or real awareness entering the picture, and energy drains away without any positive issue.

However, there is another more positive perspective on

futile conflict when there is a purpose being served. Sometimes permanent conflict is maintaining the integrity of a whole system. Thus, in a large eco-system, local and ongoing conflictual interactions between elements within it, eg. localized destruction, occasional surfeits, one species preying on another, change nothing for the whole, so from its perspective they are useful (creative), though individually destructive, and the whole thing in a state of ongoing maintained conflict.

The third outcome is creative. In *creative conflict* a productive or transformative resolution is generated by a conflictual situation. Perhaps it is a compromise, or something new, or even a useful side-effect of the very struggle to reach resolution from an energising opposition, and it makes possible a higher-level of organisation. What is destructive to one party, may be extremely creative for another. Nature relies on and flourishes from creative-destructive conflict. The tension between species erupts into active conflict as the lion seeks its prey, and the creative outcome of this conflict will nourish another generation of lions, and possibly keep the prey in balance too.

As often remarked, the serenity of an English garden is contingent upon major warfare between life seeking the same space, light and nourishment, under the ordinance of the creative will of the gardener. The more ordered the design, the higher the creative tension and the more thoroughly is destruction unleashed upon weeds, pests and unbridled growth. Wild natural landscapes achieve their own balance and beauty, but the formality of 18th century French and Italian gardens, or the exquisite order of a Zen garden is beauty of a different kind, where the ordering principles are more evident.

If esoteric principles of number and philosophy can be incorporated in the layout and planting of a garden space, it will heighten the unconscious impact, teaching without words. A group of Saros people once embarked upon the creation of an intricate Knot garden in the grounds of a large manor house we sometimes hired for courses. In the centre were plants representing the three primal forces of affirmation, denial, and unification; herbs of various kinds filled the quadrants of the four seasons, pebble and hyssop formed the borders, and the terracotta steps at each end were engraved with symbols. Working on this living mandala over the course of many weekends was an exercise in maintaining conscious attention in action, leaving a lasting impression on our souls as well as on the earth. Knot gardens are an invitation to sit and contemplate, or let the mind and feet wander over the elements of the design, imprinting it consciously and unconsciously, so they are ritualized expression.

If formal design is essentially an exercise in creative conflict, so is undertaking practical tasks with conscious attention, as opposed to the normal inward dreaming and free-flowing rumination. No mind likes being restrained from its natural associative romp, its merry-go-round of desires, feelings and thoughts, so there is always an element of conflict in attempting it. But the tension generates energy, and energy is needed to hold stillness— the space which is the inner Temple.

Which is one of the reasons why monastic traditions enshrine practical activities as part of daily routine, not just for housekeeping purposes. There may seem little practical point in polishing an already shining door-handle, sweeping a spotless floor, or raking gravel in a perfect Zen garden, but it offers a good opportunity to observe the arisings of inner conflict whilst in movement. The same could be done at home with the hoover if we set up the intention. Most effective retreats and courses incorporate daily periods of work for the community, along with an instruction along the lines of holding the mind steady, such as 'External Considering', repeating a phrase or word, or attention on breath.

And on a Saros course, should you be swinging an axe high to splinter a log, a voice might unexpectedly bellow: "STOP"! What do you do? You freeze, axe poised over your head, mouth open in a grimace of exertion. Likewise, around you, every human being present becomes a statue, poised mid-stride, mid-gesture. In a weird interval of suspended animation, only the wind continues its motion, and a bird drifts across the sky, but your awareness is suddenly sharp as a laser. You see yourself, your internal state just prior to the command, all the thoughts which were trundling around in your skull, the entire scene, the quality of the light, hear the rustle of grasses and a distant rumble of traffic. You know you are present; some internal body of aliveness is vibrating... and the axe wobbles perilously in the air. Just in time, "CONTINUE" sets the world in motion again.

That frozen moment, rife with tension, is a sacred moment of awareness, of waking up. The disciplines and exercises of group work revolve around tension, marshalling energy and the internal fire which fuses elements into a new substance. Energy is needed for any change or transformation, so the conflictual restrictions of meditation, or of any conscious task at odds with the mind's lazy flow and the ego's determination to put itself first, are always opportunity.

All in all, conflict is vital, a necessary condition for life. Glyn asserted that: 'to *maintain your own Unity, you must be at war.*' For inner work, war is a challenging metaphor, dangerously mis-interpreted by literalists. The discipline of the warrior archetype underlines the truth that real inner peace is not obtained by doing nothing, nor by giving way to the easiest impulses. Undeniably at times you have to fight your own inclinations, or outside invasions of your space and time, or nefarious undermining of your will, deliberate or circumstantial. And where there is destruction, pain, struggle, the creative can arise with new vigour and in unforeseen directions, as it did in diverse arenas from the carnage of two world wars.

> Great War-god I salute you,
> You Prodigal, you Lover in my arms!
> I speak for all the wombs of the unborn;
> Rank upon rank we wait,
> Not to scavenge petals from the earth
> Beneath your keening sword,
> But in silence, to acknowledge by blood light
> All beginnings, all life which spills itself
> On the rocky desert floor,
> That somewhere and everywhere
> by a crumbling wall, a rampart of sand,
> One other poppy may flower in the early sun.[2]

Sacrifice and Suffering

Sacrifice must be one of the oldest universal impulses: to voluntarily offer something valuable in order to receive blessing or ward off evil. In what kind of cosmos would this actually work? One view is that it is a superstitious attempt to pre-empt the unwelcome suffering visited by 'external' forces. Where our ancestors might have sacrificed a goat, or the supreme ritual sacrifice of a human being, simple cultural customs in many parts of the world still today invoke success from the cosmos through sacrifice and celebration. It is a time-honoured human impulse, and appears to be addressing a causal relationship between a human action and the non-human realm of 'otherness' (the super-natural). Many participants see it this way.

However, there is another way of looking at it, namely, as a practical method of harnessing will and intention. Fourth Way teachings as in the system of Gurdjieff, introduce the notion of intentional suffering as *deliberately adding elements of conflict to your life to support a conscious aim.* Neither is it perverse to do this—all sports people do it, musicians do it—and saints and sages choose the difficult over the easy in order to develop Being and Knowledge. The Buddha rejected extreme asceticism as a pathway to Enlightenment, but properly understood, intentional suffering can be introduced without extremes, and be as simple and effective as altering an entrenched habit for an exercise in awareness. Whether a good or bad habit, the act of changing it will produce friction and creative conflict, and thereby, your will is strengthened.

However, when we think of suffering, we usually mean the unwelcome suffering which is inflicted by fate and circumstance. Only Faith, whatever form it takes, can make unchosen suffering *intentional*, by acceptance into a framework which renders it meaningful. Faith does not necessarily relieve the suffering, but in time transforms the person, which may also transform the suffering. This is the deepest human intelligence, taught by the greatest Teachers.

We live in an age in which many seem to treat suffering as an insult to our legitimate right to well-being and comfort. Have they forgotten that in the human condition, grief, insecurity and depression are natural states cycling through most people's lives at some stage or another? Without such experience we would not be human, and we would not grow into mature understanding. It is an insidious modern fantasy to regard depressed states, unhappiness, and unsatisfactory situations as unacceptable, or abnormal, as if they somehow shouldn't happen, and should be removed. Denying, or working *against* instead of *with* these inevitable cycles of suffering compounds rather than transforms them. The result for individuals and society, may be to encourage seriously incapacitating and permanent states, anchored by pharmaceuticals, and unfortunately also by Support Networks which support the problem rather than the means to release it.

As is to be expected, for all of us the years brought their share of light and shadow. Those who know the stage described by St John of the Cross as the terrible second dark night, the Dark Night of the Spirit, may experience depression deep and lasting. The first Dark Night of the Soul is personal suffering, a necessary purification of the senses in the initial phases of inner work and approach to the Divine. The second, Purgation of the Spirit, is a stripping of everything, every faculty which intervenes to inhibit infused contemplation; death before dying, a true death of self, and the ultimate sacrifice. It is a very interior secret anguish which wears no insignia, and hidden from view, evokes no sympathy from those around. The only conscious choice is to carry on and strive to make every smallest act meaningful, every day like one's final day on earth, so that never has there been a sun so warm, a flower so vibrant, a smile on the face of a child so beautiful as on that day. Then slowly, like a cicada crawling out of its shell after seventeen years underground and drying its wings on the bark of a tree, it may become possible again to sing.[4]

Like everyone else, in the early stages I had my fair share of angst, rejections, periods of depression, and all the other emotional ups and downs which are the learning of the emotional body. I think of myself long ago as a young woman, walking the deserted Woodstock Road in Oxford in the small hours, through pools of streetlight, under autumn trees, and knowing with a strange clarity that the road would go on into the future and I must walk it, every step. For then I faced grief and my soul wanted to die, but the road stretched on ahead. I saw myself, forty years hence, looking back through years of light and shade to that moment of walking, perhaps being glad that I was still there to look back. And so I am, and it is just exactly as I foresaw in my young anguish. Though the road has changed many times, I am still walking 'the Woodstock Road' through the lamplight and the leaves, looking back and looking forward.

Glyn revealed little about his early life, but we know that his childhood was difficult and that as a young man he had some problem with alcohol at least for a period, probably until that strong drive towards Knowledge and the experience it generated took precedence. In later life although it featured rarely, he did not avoid alcohol, and I've known him share a social glass or two. On a couple of party occasions, I observed him sink more than a couple, and watched with interest to see what effect it would have. It had very little, other than conviviality. He was as sharp as ever.

I recall that on one such social occasion he instituted a party-game whereby everyone had the task of coming up with a single image to encapsulate what they saw as the essence of each person, be it an animal, an object, a public role etc. It was just for fun, of course, but it was in the aftermath of a group meeting, so I took it as a test and challenge to be accurate and insightful. I remember what I said of Glyn, because the words which emerged shocked me at the time. I looked at the challenging figure watching with a bottomless amusement from across the room, and drew deep inside my vision. Slowly I said: "You... are a Fraud".

I knew I meant it as a peculiar compliment, but I never got a chance to explain. He looked highly amused and the game moved on. Only afterwards I worked out that I was acknowledging the fact that he was not what he seemed. He always claimed to represent a Hermetic tradition, one aspect of which is the Trickster who embodies and promotes the development of wisdom but is often unrecognised. It was, in fact, a tribute to one who could write the words:

> *"Where were you when the worlds began? Where are you now? Where shall you be when your One has passed away?"*[3]

Changing the Guard

In the very early days when we were working with Cities and Temples imagery in the London group, Glyn announced cryptically: *'The Guard of the City is changing so a new Holy Temple can operate.'* What this meant was obscure to me, but I liked the sound of it—bring on the new! A physical city is a complex organization of all the functions which make up a living collective, a place of exchange and transformation in co-operation with other cities. Symbolically, we can see 'city' as representing an organisation of mind which, at the most familiar level, we know as 'I' or my-self. There are other levels of City.

The Temple is symbolically at the heart of a city, a place of concentration, dedicated to God. The nature of the perception of God depends on the level of city and temple, of which there are four in our structure, corresponding to Four Worlds which we named Structure, Flow, Rhythm and Field. There are parallels in many traditional teachings. But what could a changing of the Guard mean?

Guards defend and protect a city. In today's global 'city', many of our former defences are crumbling, such as the institutions we trusted to maintain the status quo, and the behavioural norms which governed individual actions and values. All are changing, collapsing under new pressures and tensions. To what degree is this scenario linked with the neglect of sacred values, not only in western and global society, but also in our own lives? Do we do enough to establish, let alone guard our Temple, individually and as a culture?

The destruction of the Temple in Jerusalem is a key historical and mythological motif in Jewish life, as is its restoration. Christ referred to destroying the Temple, and in three days building it up again (a temple 'not made with hands'). These are both expressions of the same theme. I choose to read Glyn's pronouncement '*...so a new Holy Temple can operate*' as a statement not just of the possible, but of the inevitable. As the nature of the City has changed, therefore the Temple at its heart must change too, but how this restoration will unfold for Humanity is not yet evident.

What is certain is that it will not be an ensemble of spiritual beliefs cherry-picked from existing religious thinkers by various committees of Worthies. That is not how the Temple operates, nor how potency coheres into meaning through the seventh pillar of consciousness. Only true vision furnishes the Temple, vision arising from the power of the Unconditioned. There is no other way.

Can we prepare for it? I feel that one practical step is to avoid the temptation to repeat and amplify the negative attitudes so relentlessly promulgated in media outlets, seemingly aimed at promoting the disintegration of world culture. In a void of sacred values, negativity can be cultured much like bacteria. We could personally resolve not to add to this proliferation by our words and attitudes.

Another suggestion is that instead of our existing *structures* of Faiths, perhaps we should look to the *space* between the structures, as an artist attends to the negative space between and around objects, or some teachings emphasize as positive non-doing, or non-thinking thinking. So, we have the space between galaxies, or space within atoms to provide us with metaphors for the noetic internal space in every human being. Knowing it, we can surpass both cultural and tribal values. Irrespective of tradition, every meditation session, and every act of conscious reflection demarcates some internal space in one's own mental and emotional clutter, and into it slips the power within silence.

Silence and darkness are the most striking aspects of the ancient underground sacred spaces—a silence so intense it vibrates, and darkness so thick you can almost touch it. But neither this silence nor darkness is oppressive. On the contrary, every sense, inner and outer, comes alive, and the *temples* on either side of the head activate. The temporal lobes in the brain are associated with the sense of time, space and hearing, all implicated in 'mystical' experience, and all relevant when standing under the earth in one of the temples of our forebears.

They are relevant too, when this kind of experience is re-created in a London flat. I once entered a room which had been cleared and sealed from all light sources late into the night. Conducted down the hallway by a guide, I was led into the darkness and left there. Silence outside, silence within and not a photon to fall on the eyes. It didn't take long before I momentarily passed out and re-emerged in the darkness in a completely different state. Space had expanded to cosmic proportions, and all Time seemed present together. Darkness and light had become indistinguishable and irrelevant to the consciousness in which I stood, feeling the universe flowing from me. Hours passed, and all too soon there was a knock on the door, and I was led into the dawning of a new day in the great Metropolis.

New Temples

One positive aspect of the bubbling cauldron of violence across the world is that it represents an upwelling of energy and force. Throughout human history the urge to create order from chaos, and beauty from rubble eventually prevails. It is a manifestation of the human spirit, and of the Universal Spirit, of whose overall designs we have not a clue. I will present an outline of temple theory in the next chapter, to show creative arising through the pillars of Love-Order, Art-Passion and Skill-Desire. It could be that we are at a very potent moment in the sacred history of the world with potential to utilize the energy of chaos to make new order, the energy of passion for beauty, and of desire for the technological skills which are already such a powerful shaper of the present.

Glyn was the inspiration behind a project which gained a little traction but was ultimately too large a conception to be realised. It was to erect a cathedral for Faith which would be a material symbol of a new religious paradigm. Known as the Deventer Project, as a reference to the 14th century lay-communities of Brothers and Sisters of the Common Life established in Deventer, Netherlands, the architect design was of an elliptical domed structure with separate elliptical cells round the central space so that it could be built anywhere in the world out of local materials, mud, grass, timber or stone. The intention was to provide a space where anyone from any religious background or none could feel at home, a sacred space for Faith beyond Faiths, beyond sectarianism. This multi-million-pound project was not achievable for us in the late twentieth century, but it seeded and grounded a grand possibility: the day when sectarian rivalries, literalist violence and small-minded doctrines could make way for humanity to make a collective statement of Faith.

Finally, a new Temple could arise from the option of humankind assuming the greater identity of People of the Galaxy, instead of People of the Earth. This is no fantasy: *we are* denizens of the Galaxy. Acknowledging our location as an allegiance, could represent a psychological shift of identity and of centre which is parallel to the impact of the Copernican revolution on the prevailing paradigm. Furthermore, what if there are other conscious races revolving round this common hub, part of the same galactic commonwealth? The potential before us is to shift our sense of identity, our religious horizons and metaphysical range in the same way that quantum dynamics is offering clues as to how to change our way of looking at what is 'real'. Chairs don't collapse under us when we realize that they are mostly empty space; we have just changed the angle of vision or way of looking at a still reassuringly solid buttock-support, and both are 'true' perceptions.

What could be the result of changing the way of looking at our greater cosmos? We could look up, or out towards the galactic centre and wonder what sort of Temple could accommodate the Faith of other conscious beings if they exist in the vastness of our common neighbourhood, as is statistically likely. The ethical and spiritual challenges of this angle of vision could be the fruitful beginnings of a new spiritual paradigm, based on the realisation that we and these other galactic beings are all family, in the same way that Earth's 'family' is Humanity. We are galactic beings – no question. Are there others out there, other temples, other representations of consciousness and divinity? Could we kneel together, meditate together, contemplate as equals the source of our common life?

It's a mythological fantasy at present! With a foundation in Principle.

---

1. See Appendix I for a diagram of the Creative and Human Octaves and how three forces interact. T.E Lawrence adapted the title of his famous book from Book of Proverbs, 9:1: "Wisdom hath builded her house, she hath hewn out her seven pillars".
2. Appendix III. To Mars
3. The Book of Jubilee, Cranswick Press
4. On the theme of what is really meant by these Dark Nights, anyone researching the more intimate life of Mother Teresa will find that she was not as the mass and popular media myth understand and like to paint her. In my view she was greater, because she struggled with her faith, as real saints do. She had made it clear that her work with the poor and dying was first and foremost training in the love of God and service for her fellow sisters for whose development she was responsible,

not a social-work operation or medical care exercise for those she served. Nor did she glide on wings of holiness achieved once by some blinding breakthrough; she struggled, like the rest of us, with her faith and internal doubt and anguish, as well as the demands of her role in the eyes of the world's media and other people's expectations. These struggles, and the holding of intention and attention on the aim, is what makes a saint, not holding sick people or organising charitable works.

Chapter 10

Gazelles

Polarity and sexuality—an esoteric understanding of Polarity as a dynamic in consciousness. The power of Two.

Because he was fascinated by the ways in which energy is created and deployed, Glyn always emphasised the importance of polarity, and proposed it as a skilful method of work. *'Our method '*, he said, *'Is to create polarities so that something can grow in the middle.'* What did he mean by this?

The first thing to note is that polarity is not merely difference or separation, but opposition and contrast, and generally the two poles need to share a natural organic root of differentiation, a pairing. A rose is not in polarity with a daffodil, nor a sofa with a chair, though they are different. Black is not polarized with any other colour than white. The unique bond between poles is how a force-field is created and transformative energy become available. Understanding and utilising polarity is all about the positive use of specific difference, bringing energies into relationship so they can interact to enliven each other while keeping separate. In this way the conditions for power are created.

Part of the challenge of working with Glyn was the fact that being purposefully subjected to the law of polarity isn't comfortable. To raise energy and promote active response Glyn would polarize people whenever possible, creating little tensions between groups in the North and South of the country, for example, or encouraging competition between strong-willed individuals who would need to sort out their differences. One instance of this was Glyn apparently giving me some helpful advice about how to handle 'my battle' with another woman over some issue or other. "You're both powerful ladies," he said, his eyes glinting. I looked at him bemused, completely unaware of having entered some affray with this other party, and was about to say, "What do you mean? What…?" when it occurred to me that he was probably doing the same with her. Therefore, I held my peace and waited, but Battle never came. However, by then I was alert, and that moment of waking up helped me to stand my ground in many circumstances over the years, and to counter my natural tendency to glide rather gormlessly into situations, sensing trouble only when it was well underway!

It is useful to purposefully raise energy by these sorts of means if there is a worthwhile context in which to deploy it—if, for instance, the individuals concerned are able to reach a new resolution, or hold onto their personal discipline and carry on working, having become aware of the game. A polarised situation can be transformed from conflict to productivity if there is either mutual dedication to a greater aim, or a powerful axis-pole. The latter is why people follow charismatic or powerful leaders who can unite differences (for good or ill). Because Glyn's integrated presence also had the effect of unifying people in his wake, he strove to counter it by the polarity principle, which forced people back onto their own resources, and their own responsibility. However, when that fails, natural tendencies and egotism can be exacerbated and the polarisation drives people apart—itself a useful outcome if the inevitable happens sooner rather than later, and within an overall structured environment. Positively or negatively, a dynamic opportunity for consciousness-raising can be created.

The Power of Two.

The dictionary defines polarity as: '*the presence or manifestation of two opposite or contrasting principles or tendencies. The condition of having poles.*' A polarised situation creates a Field, which is an invisible structure of forces, tensions, balances and flows.

Our entire western civilization is based on harnessing the energetic relationship between two opposite poles of electromagnetic energy. In the psycho-sphere, the polarity between light and dark, good and evil, yin and yang, masculine and feminine underpins philosophy, metaphysics, morality and life itself in sex and conception, and religion can be polarised into transcendent Divinity and immanent indwelling Divinity. According to Glyn's principle, from a faithful struggle to make either religious position into real experience, what can grow in the middle is *realization* or *liberation*. Paradoxically, it is ultimately liberation from polarisation, from the bondage of a polarised view, for the way to resolve paradox is the 'yes' in the middle.

I'm sure I don't need to elaborate the principle of polarity itself, but it is not so often seen in quite such a utilitarian fashion as a technique for raising consciousness. Consciousness is not 'raised' like a lump of dough by kneading it directly. It is better to conceive of it as energy, illumined energy, and therefore the trick is to establish poles (indirectly) so 'something' can grow in the middle, of itself, by its own inherent power. Creative illumination (consciousness) may increase slowly and imperceptibly, or as an 'influx', but either way it is a manifestation of freedom not contrived or controlled by personal will. It is a 'Supreme Event' beyond polarity, arising in a temple space created for it.

Recognising and utilising the value of opposition, and of tension and conflict is a novel approach compared with holistic philosophy which promotes a vision of wholeness and harmony as not only the goal, but the *means* of 'consciousness raising'. Harmony is not useful as a means, rather the contrary. Harmony may be the *product*, the outcome of two forces in relationship or opposition, and is a force in itself only if it becomes the leading force in further interaction (third force). In this way three forces eternally interact as the dynamic of all creation.

An esoteric philosophy which is explicitly based on polarisation is the Kabbalistic Tree, structured on the polarity of two side 'pillars'. The right pillar is expansive, wisdom/mercy, and the left balances it with judgement/severity. Both are essential to life and consciousness, and the interplay creates triads of interaction, balances and imbalances experienced through consciousness as the middle 'pillar'. Similarly, all forms of prayer, meditation, and spiritual exercises which collect energy otherwise expended in the dissipative pursuits of daily living, are polarising our personal sense of identity with a greater: God, the True Self, the real 'I'. We struggle not to waste energy by negativity and negative states. We rein in the wandering mind. We juxtapose the ideal with the real, and end up somewhere in the middle, but more conscious.

Love and Sex

Now to sex. Since my first draft of this chapter, sex and gender have become a lot more controversial, and I have watched with some astonishment the two poles of human-ness being forcibly re-engineered and obliterated in some sections of the public mind. With it, the root symbolism of the Temple.

Human sexuality has a complex span with physical, emotional and mental constituents, but all three are involved in the states of *desire, passion* and *love* which are recognisably distinct expressions on the sexual spectrum. Naturally they are intertwined, and in the throes of a powerful sexual attraction, who cares about such distinctions? Until something goes wrong. Then it may become all too painfully clear that the lovers were operating on different axes: the separate driving forces of a complex state. Sexuality is a potent force, like the sacred Temple, sharing common roots with it in the depths of the psyche.

The level of abstract Temple relevant to this discussion has pillars created by the three basic forces of Desire, Passion and Love polarised with Skill, Art and Order respectively, through which each can fruitfully be expressed.

The logic is that *Love* grows and is sustainable through establishing some sort of *order*, framework or context, whether it be a partnership like marriage, or the responsibilities of family and work, or any enterprise begun and maintained for love's sake.

Passion demands expression. It is energetic and can be short-lived but channelled creatively it gives rise to *art*, expressing its fire and inspiration through genius, innovation, or painting, music, literature etc.

Desire is a driver, an insistent and essential motivator for all action, and it's the reason we acquire *skills* of any kind and have patience to develop them.

In due proportion, the urges of desire, passion and love

inspire and sustain the deepest sexual relationships, and flower also in the religious impulse, directed towards the Divine and the love of God ('bhakti' in Sanskrit). Without the motivation of desire, nothing in the living world would move; desire drives the engine of creation. Desire for God is poignantly expressed in the entire world's spiritual literature, and in great laments like the Psalms. Passion is a fire which burns and brings suffering ('passion' means suffering), as in the Passion of Christ, or any overwhelming emotional drive. Great Love may cover the whole spectrum of emotional possibility, including mystical love, and engage body as well as mind and heart. The world's great sacred erotic hymns like the Song of Solomon, and mystical love poetry in every tradition, are interpreted as *secular* seductions to those uninitiated into the mysteries of spiritual love. However, the truth is more subtle.

Personally, I had resolved when very young that until I could 'know' the reality, the truth of it, it would be impossible to 'love' some Divine Being I had essentially fabricated from my desire. Later I came to appreciate that Love in a spiritual context is not necessarily the same as powerful feelings, nor the emotion and passion associated with human sexuality. On the other hand, what about all that erotic love-based mystical literature of the great traditions? What about Bernini's famous erotic statue of St Teresa where the saint's inner experience of ecstasy is vividly conveyed through her posture? (Apparently, she also had a tendency to levitate in her ecstasies, and would wedge her feet, or ask the other nuns to sit on her to curb the uncontrollable manifestation of her body.)

Even before I knew it, I suspected that the *earthly* was a reflection of the *heavenly*, not, as popularly assumed, the other way around. Of course, it's natural to assume that human sexual love is being extolled under the guise of religious mysticism, given that it can be the most transporting experience commonly available. But how else could one describe *divine* love, when the available language and imagery is *human* experience of desire, passion and love at its most intense? Symbolism always works this way, the concrete and literal being a shadow of something more ineffable, and pointing by analogy to something more abstract (though no less real). We have to rely on our senses, both outer and inner, to register and define form and figure.

> *"If you would seek the imperceptible, seek first the perceptible"*[1]

The perceptible constitutes evidence, but *"do not lose yourself"* is the counsel.

Religious mysticism and practices ranging from asceticism to Tantra address the challenge of the physical body from different directions, one trying to overcome it, the other diving deep into somatic experience. The full range of psycho-physiology, energy systems and subtle anatomy only becomes experiential through some form of conscious work and training. Sexual energy is the root force of all energy. It is vital to recognize its role and power to destroy or create on many levels, not just physical, and certainly not just genital sex. Mystical, ecstatic transports are whole-body phenomena; hence Bernini's St Teresa has caught the experience of rapture.

Mystical love approaches *adoration*, qualitatively different from the reciprocal nature of ordinary love; self-transcendent, translucent and rare. I remember an injunction from the nuns of my schooldays: "Adoration belongs to God alone." They were exactly right. But of course, they also unwisely banned the use of the word 'adore' in any other more casual context. This was tough to police with a bunch of exuberant adolescent girls, and descended into farce along with a (possibly apocryphal) ban on patent leather shoes in case they reflected our underwear.

Our group formed around Glyn when most of us were in our 20's and 30's, so sexual relationship was an issue. Glyn himself was faithfully married with two children, and the family were frequently present in the kitchen for the ongoing discussions, his children displaying a precocious interest and talent for argument early on. It was an example most of us followed, and given the teaching that polarising the sexes is a bountiful source of energy needed to pursue the aims of the Work, sexual indulgence and not taking responsibility for one's sexual behaviour would be unskilful and wasteful. Glyn once said of himself, that he worked best in group activities with a woman for whom he was aware of a sexual attraction, a 'buzz'. It was fine to acknowledge buzz; not fine to take it personally and act on it in the usual ways.

Partnerships formed and re-formed among the community we were, but Glyn was always watchful, and ready to advise on problems, treating them as an opportunity for insight and education. Besides which, sex was a powerfully interesting subject for discussion, study and observation. Genuine objectivity is an excellent defence against misbehaviour. Many communities and teachers have faltered on the rocks of 'detachment', having interpreted it as restriction (or license) without understanding the consequences of a context which raises energy.

Discipline raises energy, restriction acts as a compressor, and without the knowledge of how to direct energy into productive channels, the result is sexual pressure leading to misadventures. Productive channels in a community of meditators, for instance, might be physical work like chopping wood or carrots, challenging the intellect with meaningful tasks, or working at expression in art, dance or music, but probably not directing the increased energy simply into more *determined* meditation. To generate energy through spiritual practices without recognising the impact on individuals (at their varying stages of development) is a recipe for trouble. Maturity and stability in the spiritual life develop slowly, under wise guidance and/or study.

So, we attempted to educate ourselves and learn the ways of it. I remember a day when I went through quite a lot of men. It was an exercise in raising and handling sexual energy, and we were set up in a series of pairs or fours in a large room to polarise with an opposite gender to the best of our ability, but *without moving*. I gazed deep into the eyes of my partner, and tried summoning up sexual energy from just about every part of my anatomy: come-hither eyes, Mona Lisa smirks, the faintest twitch of a leg. It definitely worked better with some men than others. This was interesting. With some partners it was like trying to connect with a brick wall. With others there was a current, but it was hard to detect what made the difference. It was something in the atmosphere, in the field between us; energies even subtler than body-language in the absence of movement.

Gazelles

The materialist sex-obsessions of our age are fuelled by egocentricity. Sex is awesome, its power is the basis of all creativity and life itself, and its destructive potential equally terrifying. A poem I wrote many years ago which has given the title to this chapter, expresses the paradox of what we have forgotten about this power, and I don't think I can say it any better. It is worth a short excursion and homage to the bigger picture before a more prosaic account of my own life journey.

There is tension between vast generative power and the delicate receptivity of life.

Your harness, Love, and the wheels of your power like suns
Will make of me a wide, wide pasture where gazelles from the desert
Can come and graze by night.

Night always symbolizes the closing of the senses, the enclosure of meditation, and the potency of darkness. Desert is the wilderness of the lost, thirsty heart searching for meaning in an impermanent universe.

But there's an underlying threat and danger in the power and deep root of sexual energy, some wild, potentially inimical power in the desert itself causing dunes to boom (a phenomenon known in sandy desert landscapes).

They say when even wind withholds,
The dunes are heard to boom:
The desert ululates her daemon-lover.

And in the midst of this dark power, or indeed out of it, comes life: the delicately fragile beauty of new birth and of small and tender creatures, "shy-eyed herds":

In sleeping fields, the dark-rimmed animals
Are listening, stepping lightly as the moon
To milk the faintest sounds within the earth.

Those gazelles stand for interior attune-ment, that which listens, which can hear subtleties, the inner not the outer ears. It is the inner listening which is engaged in meditation, and meditation, along with all development of the inner bodies of our total psychic anatomy, is a refinement of sexual energy. Paradoxically, with refinement comes power, a force which can break through creatively, but not without the effort of 'reining in the living creatures' of thoughts and desires, and sometimes not without cataclysm— the fierce potential of Love to break open the heart.

Until the living creatures come to rein,
And Earth and I, your minions, split like pods.

(See Appendix III for the complete poem[2].)

Life lessons

At the age of twenty I decided with the passionate intensity of the young, that in my dotage I wanted to be able to look back and say that I had 'loved much'. Not for me to end up some shrivelled old prune! My logic was that something as powerful and interesting as love and sex might need some learning; that the ability to love might accumulate with practice. However, although the sexual revolution was in full swing in the seventies and eighties, I managed to avoid a rampage, probably because I did not confuse love and sex.

My first great passion was entirely unrequited but full of inspiration and longing. I followed it literally across the world, when the love of my life re-located from Australia to Europe. I had an address, and a strong intent. Armed with these I managed to turn up by a series of totally serendipitous 'accidents' of circumstance at the door of a flat in an industrial town in Germany, and not just once, but three times before I found him at home. Looking back on it, I see a remarkable exercise of will, transporting me by chance connection not just to the region, but the precise town, and not least because Circumstances had to arrange for three 'accidental' passings-by.

I did not have to force any of it. Chance seemed to conspire with me nicely. Many years later in Oxford, when I kept running into someone I thought I was trying to avoid, I remarked on the frequency of these unintended encounters to Glyn during one of his visits. He commented wryly: "You think it's accident? You're doing it." Oh! It was a lesson on the unconscious power of will, which can fasten on an object, and actually works best without 'conscious' manipulation or desire.

So, astonished at finding me blown 10,000 miles into his path, my first Great Love took me for coffee. As I stirred in the cream, I knew with a contraction of the heart that we would part in that little German cafe, and that would be it. We said goodbye outside, and I walked away from years of hopeful dreams. As I sat waiting for the train on the empty platform, a cuckoo called from the woods opposite, and I wrote in the dust with a stick: 'Let him go'. And then the bands lifted; I was free. When the train arrived, I left him behind with the dust.

My second Great Love walked into a symbolic dream I had as a small child. I never forgot this simple dream, because I was sure that I would know that man when I encountered him, one day, when I grew up. Many years later, when a man I had just met insisted on accompanying me shopping in the

Oxford covered market, I turned around to see him enacting the gesture in the same way and circumstances that I had seen so long ago in my dream. The world literally turned sideways for an instant. All the fruit on the stalls, especially the oranges, glowed with colour. It was one of those moments of expanded perception which are life-changing. I had actually noticed a strange mood or power in the air the evening before as I crossed Magdalen Bridge to the event where I met him. In retrospect it was a premonition of things to come. The power from these portents, and the eventual suffering of abandonment when the relationship came to a painful end, directly led me into the Work.

The wheel kept on turning. Others entered my life and left it, but each time I gained and grew, and a descent into prunehood was fortuitously avoided.[3]

But then one afternoon I sat in Glyn's kitchen discussing astrology and the suitability of opposites, like Scorpio and Taurus. "Bless you, my children" said Glyn with an ironical gleam, indicating myself (scorpio) and the young man with the Fiat (taurus). No Scorpio can bypass an innuendo like that! The train to Oxford was just clearing the rail-yards of Paddington Station when it hit me. "On no…Not…!." An incipient cold immediately took root, and I spent the weekend in bed, wrestling with feverish energies as body and psyche tried to adjust to the notion Glyn had planted in such an offhand manner. That was how marriage and children finally entered my life, just as I had solemnly resolved to bow to the looming fate of Bluestocking. Another perception had come to me on the Paddington train: a pre-vision of this man standing beside me in a hospital bed as I held a dark-haired blue-eyed baby boy. It also came to pass.

Balance

Balance is never static. Sexual polarity is like the balance which exists at the fulcrum of a see-saw, or at the centre of the rope in a tug-of-war. Despite all the force being exerted on both sides, the centre is perfectly still, a stillness which is the result of powerful momentum, of the potentiality of equal movement held in check. Balance is forces in equilibrium, not the absence of force. The centre is the generative point, pure potential, the creative heart of the Temple.

Because esoteric science promotes a deeper understanding of gender, to help build sexual dynamism, at one stage the men got themselves together and went off on wild-men expeditions on the moors, trudging around, challenging themselves to survive a night without maps etc. Some men enjoyed this; others hated it, but all learned something from the opportunity to observe and recognise their own reactions.

We women organised ourselves from early on. For me personally, from childhood, far from feeling oppressed or suffering penis-envy, I used to marvel at the great good fortune of having been born female, quite certain that femaleness offered so much more magic and mystique and was so much more interesting, varied and *deep* than maleness! I wondered how far into this mystery my life would take me, and it was a thread I had to follow into many years of discussion and work with other women, through which we explored the roots of the feminine.

In the early years of Saros, Glyn's presence and approach was strong. He generated a high-energy, robust, totally unsentimental and abstract field, which on one seminal course left me feeling obscurely but deeply out of sync with an energy which seemed the epitome of male dynamics. I went around other women trying to ascertain if they felt similarly. I never doubted the value of this powerful field, but something in my nature sought to counter-balance it with a different energy of working. I linked this with a root which I felt needed to be acknowledged and explored—the nature of being Woman, and so a female working group formed. Glyn supported this development absolutely and gave 'technical' advice whenever it was sought, but insisted it was not his area, and he could not make any connection with the work which arose and drew on a female lineage and approach to spiritual aspiration.[4]

When once I asked him what to do when sexual energy is raised in the context of esoteric work, he replied: '*escalate, but hold the reins of the disciplines to steer the chariot*'.[5] The discipline aspect of spiritual work is designed precisely to handle powerful energies and steer them in a fruitful and creative direction, which is why personal conduct and self-responsibility are so important—they are tools to handle power which can move the soul and open the doors of perception.

It is probably true that a celibate or monastic life allows for a much greater concentration of root energy for development of the inner life, but at the same time the potential for mis-direction, repression or unhealthy psychological states is great in such a specialist life-style. Our approach was to look for principles operating in everyday life and use the unruliness of living in the world to try and act at least with integrity, if not with wisdom. Most of us were in reasonably stable marriages or partnerships and raised families. For morality, we had the precept of self-responsibility—that you are responsible for your own thoughts, words and actions— which covers most eventualities and leaves no wiggle room. To it can be added the irrefutable: '*One action, one result. Another action, another result*', and Glyn's favourite slogan '*No such thing as a free lunch*'.

1. The Book of Jubilee
2. Appendix III. Gazelles
3. Appendix III. The Mothers
4. The Circle of Nine, Gilchrist, Weiser 2018 was developed in this context
5. The imagery of riding the Chariot is found in the Merkabah tradition in Kabbalism, and the chariot allegory in Plato's Phaedrus.

Chapter 11

End

How I set about seeing what practical clues I could find for unlocking the Gates of Life and Death.

Renaissance paintings sometimes show a skull sitting on the desk of a philosopher, suggesting a morbid preoccupation or gothic fascination with death and corruption. However, in this context it was actually a statement that a true philosopher needs to take death into the foundation of both his life and his philosophy. The skull served to remind of two things: that remaining aware of life's end is an incentive and goad to make it truly alive while you have it, and that there are tactical means for cultivating this 'aliveness'. Also, that Life without Death is fantasy. It does not exist.

As average persons we generally choose avoidance as a day to day strategy, which works well enough, mostly. Other chosen responses include hedonism or asceticism. Hedonism, stuffing as much sensory experience into every moment as possible, is a strategy which actively evades the underlying questions, but the short-term gain is precarious, subject to shocks and reversals outside one's control (ie. death). Extreme asceticism is an insurance policy, buying into death early by attempting to strangle aspects of life in order to reach the state promised beyond it. The Buddha tried this, but gave it up as a bad deal.

Yet I instinctively felt that without taking account of death, life is simply shapeless, hedged about with an intimation of being merely a snippet of something ever so much larger, but of what? When I started instructing people in meditation it troubled me because I thought to myself: "What if someone asks me about death? What can I say *from my experience?*" I had a valid method to pass on, I had some theoretical structure for the mind, but not *knowledge* of this inescapable mystery.

And of course, it was not long before a terrible test occurred. A meditator rang me and in a broken voice, sheered with anguish, told me her son had been killed in a car accident on the other side of the world. Given all the meditation she had done and her devotion to prayer, the burning question for her was, when it happened "why didn't I *know*? We were so close..." She expected to have felt it, to have an intimation of the rupture. I had no answer then, and it haunts me still.

Shocked, I went to sit under the apple tree in late autumn sunshine and asked myself the same question. All that meditation and spiritual work, and not a ripple travelled through the subtle cosmos to alert her to the passing of her son. That silence was brutal. It was a defining moment which made me ask myself what I actually knew about death, and the sheet came up blank. I had a lot of very comprehensive theory and philosophy—of worlds and cosmoses and their generation and inter-relationship, the role of Man in vast cycles and octaves, and all of it about life and death and all of it deeply illuminating to the mind—but when it came to a simple statement to advise a grieving person, or a person nearing death, what could I say with authenticity?

As for my own death, like many, if not most people at some stage of their life, I had known the sort of loss or misery which makes one visit the idea of ending one's own life, or at least long for the release and cessation of suffering it seems to represent. I had a romantic idea in youth that the one thing no one could take from you was the 'right' to your own death. That darkly comforting illusion bit the dust the day I got close enough to contemplate it. I saw with mounting horror the reality of an interconnected cosmos in which the consequences of an act of life-denying cowardice were likely to reverberate into spheres beyond my conception. I sensed, rather than could articulate, the awesomeness and horror it could unleash for myself and others. As with the old adage 'out of the frying pan into the fire', with every fibre of my being and on every level, I knew the fire was a bad choice. That was a very low point for me—discovering that we have no rights over our death.

In those days I hadn't thought very deeply about life and death and didn't know anything about karma, but it was blindingly clear to some intuitive sense that there was no escape by trying to opt out. How could I opt out of an immense and mysterious process of which I knew nothing, except that *here I was*? I knew neither the beginning nor the end, nor what kept the whole great cycle of creation turning. All I knew with a visceral sense was that bad choices have bad consequences. And probably worse than anything of which I could conceive at that point in my development.

As part of my quest to know death, at one point I became a Hospice volunteer. Here death was treated with compassion and warmth, and in my mind the hospice became a kind of Way-station to the Eternal, with regular departures for the Unknown. But though I sat with many people in the last days and weeks of their lives, we were trained to be listeners, not to proffer any views of our own, or step where we might disturb the delicate process of a person's own way of dealing with their situation. So, it was not really an engagement, more an accompaniment. The experience underlined for me a sense of how death is a natural presence within life, and of the holiness and mystery surrounding each individual death as if a powerful sacred space was breaking through into the mundane. It is why death has such an atmosphere of the numinous for observers, touching deeply those who are present. But I also observed the slightly surprising, and surprisingly ordinary fact, that as a general rule, people die as they have lived.

It may happen in some cases, but generally it seems that a person's attitudes and expectations don't change radically even when faced with the impending end of all they have known, and the unknown beyond. So, as all spiritual work advocates, death is best explored well before the end looms. "Remember now thy Creator, in the days of thy youth, while the evil days come not, nor the years draw nigh when thou shalt say, I have no pleasure in them;" (Ecclesiastes 12.1)

Some years later I worked as a professional Funeral Arranger, responsible for arranging life's final ritual. A funeral is one of the last remaining sacred rituals in modern life. A funeral usually opens the doors of the other world a little, not just because of the powerful emotion present, but because the emotion is channelled, modulated through ceremony, with dignity, restraint, solemnity and usually a nod to the bigger dimension. I helped set such a context for families, some of whom had never darkened the door of a church, but still wanted to send off their loved one from a sacred space. The long-suffering local vicar was therefore called in to do the honours. Others maintained a Humanist philosophy, but they also called in a professional to give the ceremony weight and solemnity. When emotion is strong, the channelling effect of properly conducted ritual is obvious.

A good funeral is more than a bit moving—it literally moves Heaven and Earth, briefly intertwining the two realms. However, I observed one interesting phenomenon. As a funeral arranger I sometimes knew when a death was a suicide by the chaos which seemed to accompany it. Doorbells didn't work, flower orders went wrong, timings and bookings got screwed up. Everything was difficult, as if the field around this death was scrambled, and the mourning of the family was heavy as a weight.

Narratives

Obviously, the meaning of death is not penetrated from studying its outer manifestations, and a meaningful logic for death and after-death is offered through religious doctrines, narratives and sacred myths which are cogent, explanatory and a stabilizing foundation for making life-choices. Of the three main camps, the Judeo-Christian approach centres on one single lifetime leading to an after-life 'somewhere else' which is determined by actions in that lifetime. The Eastern model, in various formulations, proposes a progression through many lifetimes related to the choices made while living and the lessons learned by so doing, until an ultimate perfect release from the whole cycle. Then there is a pragmatic view, agnostic or humanist, which declines to speculate or consider any aftermath of the current lifetime.

Symbolically, there is no right or wrong in the alternative

views. They are different understandings of life and death, meaningful to those who hold them. In addition, a persuasive narrative is becoming increasingly well-documented, namely, direct experiential reports. These include near-death experiences (NDE's), spiritualism, after-death contact experiences, moment of death visitations, reincarnation accounts and other paranormal occurrences. All such experiences involve a change of state or consciousness. And so, we get a little nearer to articulating the real mystery at the heart of death: *Consciousness.*

What is Consciousness/Awareness? With death providing a lens, we can keep it simple and factual, side-stepping any sophisticated neuro-physiological and philosophical speculation from Consciousness Studies, or the elaborate analyses of traditional metaphysical theory. The simple and personal experiential truth is this: since we don't know how consciousness arose in our own situation at the beginning of life, we cannot *in our own experience* determine what might happen at death. A new-born is immediately conscious, but where or how did that consciousness arise? We can't answer any 'where', 'why', 'how' or 'what' questions. All we can say is *we have the experience*, and every single human being has the experience of consciousness, integrally and wholly.

Despite brave scientific and dogmatic attempts, we cannot ever examine consciousness as an object, dissecting, dividing, or setting boundaries, because consciousness cannot be located objectively. We just see where it operates, subjectively. Science is catching up with the subjective, but the limits are axiomatic.

Wordy discussions about the mysteries of consciousness inevitably rest on imagery and analogy, because the principle is invisible. Some spiritual teachings express this directly and clearly; others wrap up their approach in myth and symbol. We can also note that conscious awareness is not 'homogenous', and through training and practice awareness can be increased/extended from the base-consciousness common to us all. The fact that some are more attuned to finer states of awareness or perception than others, accounts for the fact that there are different narratives of death and the beyond. Great prophets and sages may see and understand truths which are closed to the ordinary man and woman, and will frame their experience in their contemporary context and language.

The same applies to NDE's and present-day experiences: the description will owe its character to the conscious awareness of the experiencer, his or her personal paradigm or the prevailing milieu, which in the West is often humanist. Yes, something powerful has occurred, but we don't actually know the totality we are dealing with, so the content of the experience is not the 'Truth' in any absolute sense. Communicating it to others has to rely on metaphor and image.

My father had a series of TIA's (transient ischaemic attacks) before his eventual death from a stroke, and I remember him describing his first one to me in a wondering voice. He was puzzled by what was happening in his body and mind as paralysis took hold, but he noticed he was still there calmly watching it all. He found the separation between 'himself the watcher' and what was occurring very intriguing, and I'm sure this experience and fore-knowledge contributed to his peaceful exit when his time finally came to be united with that 'other self', the one who was aware.

Glyn had suffered a heart-attack and brush with death some years previously, but at that time my attempts to probe for some nugget of insight from him about his experience had only produced a glint in the eye and a favourite phrase: "It *concentrates the mind wonderfully*!"

In the week before his death, realising that time was running out to learn direct from this source, I went back to the hospital two days in a row, with the idea of trying to 'see' or gauge where he was at, even if he said nothing to enlighten me. He said nothing and I saw nothing. It was never possible to lead him where he did not wish to go! Perfectly compos mentis, he was watching a little television and manipulating his tetrahedron made of ping-pong balls, but either in pain or 'in some other space', he said little. However, I suspect he guessed I'd come with a purpose, because when I got up to leave, in an unaccustomed gesture, he took my hand and gave it a squeeze, as if to say: "Never mind, Girl. You'll find out one day."

Knowledge itself cannot be given, or passed on. Only the Way to knowledge, the method, can be transmitted to others. By this criterion, uncovering the meaning of death and dying is an individual quest, an effort not to cleave to a dogma, but to work at growth in understanding '*Answers close doors; questions open them*'. He said this so often, and therefore was kind enough not to feed me any ready answer about death, leaving the whole issue as a potent force in life, a gigantic cattle-prod for my bovine nature.

Testimony

There is one rule of thumb, which most of us sensibly employ anyway for areas outside our own experience. Glyn expressed it as looking to '*the testimony of worthy persons*'. When it comes to important matters, (death is quite important), it is highly prudent to evaluate the *source* of information if we are unable or ill-equipped to assess the validity of the content. If we accept someone's authority in a particular area, it should be after a little active investigation as to whether they are truly in a position to testify, rather than because they happen to be in a position of authority, or because lots of people believe the same, or because one is too lazy to look further into the matter! 'Worthy' signifies a person qualified to attest because of their expertise, which includes maturity and insight, the latter being particularly important apropos of death and the spiritual.

Given that death appears to us personally as a great Unknown, the testimony of others may be the best way to approach it. Aside from experiencing the loss and death of loved ones, or having a near-brush oneself, there are other avenues to learn something of value. For the philosopher, a skull sitting on the desk can be saying: "Your death is yours to own, and to turn into an asset if you choose." After all, is there anything—literally *anything*—as certain as Death in this shifting universe? Death is the most powerful and in-your-face *certainty* in the universe, and certainty should be a powerful resource. If you were *certain* your house was going to burn down, you would take some steps would you not?

The method, according to ancient wisdom, is to 'die before you die'. If *you 'dies'*—ie. the personal, the impermanent, the limited—what is left? Is there an i*mmortal self,* or *no self* to be found? Asked this, I'm sure Glyn would reply: 'Yes'! It is said that when Christ the saviour died, the veil of the Temple was torn. What does the tearing of this veil mean in the context of Temple-symbolism, and what might be revealed? It is a sort of *koan* worth contemplating. Fifteenth century manuals, A*rs Moriendi,* gave advice on the art of dying, and prescribed the attitudes and practices for a good death.

We know that the practice of meditation rehearses the journey. As states of awareness change, awareness of the body too changes. The practitioner is faced with the question: when the mind is no longer thinking, and the body is quiescent, *who* is observing? Is it the same '*who*' navigating the bardos of Tibetan Buddhism? The bardos describe in colourful cultural imagery a series of stages one might pass through in the dying process, including some graphic portrayals of horrors one may encounter. The 'horrors' are resistances of various kinds. With recognition, they are overcome and death is serene, just as a meditator slips into 'samadhi', a state of serenity and unity when the breath seems to stop. Death is called 'mahasamadhi', the great samadhi (mind-together) in Buddhism and Hinduism, because this time breath does not resume.

Because the visionary experience of individuals gave rise to and shaped the teachings about death in the great religious traditions, the best of the teaching remains as the '*collective testimony of many worthy persons*', notwithstanding the specific mythological and cultural context. Unfortunately, the real kernel of experiential truth is often largely obscured by generations of believers adding simplistic or literal interpretations to the corpus. For instance, reincarnation is far subtler than someone re-appearing as an insect or having been Cleopatra in a previous life. How the ancient, and some would claim, universal doctrine of re-birth is interpreted will depend on the metaphysics of the culture and the insight of the transmitter. And always there are enigmatic manifestations of the supernatural to challenge rationality, as in re-incarnating Tibetan Lamas, and children who recognise a family from their previous life.

Glyn's view is probably reflected in the Spindle of Necessity myth which I described in the context of the Temple. In this

Platonic version of Karma, souls returning from one life choose the next according to previous experience, and it is likely to be a foolish or habitual choice unless they cultivate attention and learn the lessons of their previous lifetime. They pass through the hands of the three Fates who measure, spin and cut the threads of life, singing of the past, present and future. The three are the daughters of Necessity, and the soul must pass beneath Lady Necessity on her throne before drinking of the Waters of Lethe (forgetfulness) and continuing the journey into a fresh existence. There's also a random element, a lottery, which is a reminder of the existence of a third force in any choice. Life does not shuttle us mechanically between forces of duality; there is always a third option.

More originally, Glyn came up with various other interesting rationales for re-incarnation. One I have noted was an analogy of each 'oneness' (an individual) being like an electro-magnetic field, which propagates by resonance. When one field collapses back into the Unconditioned, the memory can propagate into another when the conditions are similar. He saw creation always as a process of continual re-generation, re-germination.

Then there was the Compost theory, the Digestor. I'm sorry to say I can't do justice to this, but I present these fragments because there are others who better understand the abstract background of principle, for which Glyn's originality constantly strove to find a suitable analogy. He supposed that at death, all four levels of human existence (eg. physical, intellectual, emotional, progenitive) collapse and fall into their *negative image*, which cancels out their energy and allows newness to arise. Everything generates a negative image. The ultimate recycling is when the *forms* of Life return to the absolute *no-thing* from which they arose, and from that consciousness, new

Life comes forth, eternally. Life is not the same as consciousness.

It makes experiential sense. This constant reversal, falling back and rising, from nowhere to nowhere, is our actual experience of life and nature. A child appears. A grandparent disappears. That's the experience, without explanation. We know it also when we deeply contemplate or meditate, and accept no image, embrace no-thing. It is like a little death, and from it arises a new quality of living, new insight, new being, a creative influx. Glyn also saw meditation as a sort of digestive process working to cleanse the mind of all its rubbish and decomposing it so it can be recycled.

It's true this approach to re-incarnation seems to overlook the *personal*, and leaves little scope for one's personal self to return rejuvenated in a fresh body for another round of living, so I doubt the Digestor theory will become popular. But then, neither is any true understanding of the self in relationship to Infinity because it has to be earned. Knowledge is a work in progress for most of us.

With a little understanding, one can accept that Heaven is not a place in the clouds, or a paradise full of virgins, nor is Hell a cavern with flames and pitchforks. And yet, here's the thing—perhaps you, like me, have felt those 'pitchforks'? I've personally encountered demons aplenty, I know the 'flames' of torment and I recognise the anguish of an eternal separation from God. I've also known moments of beauty or joyousness for which there is no better word than 'Heaven'. So, heaven and hell are as real as any other experience in life, part of our experiential lexicon. In life and death, we have no evidence to contradict the reasonable supposition that consciousness is present in both.

Passing

When we encounter death personally, a breath of the beyond enters the mundane world. The moment when the rhythm of breath stills is awesome. Few observers are immune to the touch of the intangible at this moment, and many report changes in the light or other phenomena which they remember forever as marking the moment of passing.

I will conclude with an account of two significant deaths in my own life, of my father and Glyn, though at neither was I physically present.

When my father lay dying on the other side of the world, something mysteriously interrupted the routine of dinner with my children. At that time, I was living with my husband and our two young children in a London flat when I was phoned by my family in Australia to say that my father had had a stroke and was unconscious in hospital. The prognosis was not good. For a day or so I carried on with family life, aware of my dear father probably near death so far away at the other side of the world. Even then I was intuitively aware enough of death issues to say to my mother by phone: "Tell Dad to think of the sun setting behind the Otways (mountains he loved and had spent much of his life gazing at), and go with the light."

She did not get the chance to tell him. The next evening in London I was having dinner with my young family when I suddenly felt queer. Not ill, just as if my digestive system was shutting down making it difficult to take in food. I struggled on for a while not wishing to make a fuss or disrupt routine, but then I had to make excuses and go away by myself.

I had barely settled into a quiet space, when I felt my father, full of bewilderment and confusion. I calmed and embraced him and, as it were, took his hand, and together we walked towards the soft radiating light. At a certain point I knew I could go no further and he must go on alone. Therefore, I let go, and simply pointed in the direction of the light which had become a powerful, white radiance. There was a moment of parting, and my father left me, moving towards the Light.

The phone call came early next morning, London time. My father had passed away during the Australian night: they weren't sure of the exact time. But I knew. I did some calculations and realised that the time I had been with my father would have been about three a.m. in the morning Downunder. It didn't matter that my mother had not been able to pass on my message. He had got it anyway.

This *Requiem for my Father* is my memorial:

Death will come with the night wind from the stars,
Treading softly, the universe in its wings,
And touching you will whisper 'Come'.
We shall rise up, you and I, and follow
Through the gate into a mighty plain.
No star shines here but one, enormously.
Bewildered, you alone must go into the light
To meet your destiny, while I remain
To honour you, my father, and point towards eternity.

As Glyn finally approached his own end, he seemed unbothered, having been preparing and hinting for some years that he was ready to go. Right up to the day of his death he remained lucid and tried to convey matters of insight to people gathered round his bed.

As I sat with my husband on the other side of his bed that final day, Glyn struggled with some animation and urgency to clarify the significance of the dreidel at Hanukkah, which is linked with the re-dedication of the Temple. He had mentioned these themes shortly before, and I had done a little research, but the vehemence with which he tried to impress some significance on us just as he prepared to leave the world, was surprising. I knew these were probably the last words I would hear him speak, and I leaned over the bed, straining to catch every syllable and to understand. At the time it was obscure. It has taken many years before I have some glimmers of understanding.

The dreidel is a spinning top` with a very old European history (including in England and Ireland as a 'teetotum', a word meaning 'the whole') and pre-dating its Jewish incarnation. It is a version of the Spindle of Necessity, with the same significance of the revolving wheel of the cosmos. Around the whorl revolve all things, and all spheres. Perhaps he was aware that he would soon face the choice, to return or to be free, as he slipped towards the river of Forgetfulness. I have no doubt he was referring to this aspect, not so much for himself, but to hammer it into our consciousnesses, because he also specifically emphasized the importance of re-dedicating the Temple, and curiously it seemed then, he stressed the fact that it is a *children's* game at Hanukkah, the Festival of Lights.

The dreidel has four sides: *All, Nothing, Take away, Put down*. As a game, depending on which side falls uppermost, one either puts in, takes out or does nothing. Our fate may be to receive all, nothing, or a part, but we also need to give. Wholeness, perhaps our happiness, depends on the spin and fall of the Top at any moment. And who spins the Top?

The festival of Hanukkah celebrates the re-dedication of the Temple, and its restoration after a period of being taken over and desecrated. We can read the symbolism universally, as I'm sure Glyn did, and finally I understood why his last words to us were to accentuate the importance of establishing and maintaining the Temple, as I have discussed at some length in Chapter 9. It was his life's work, and it was in the forefront of his mind as death crept upon him. Children are the next generation, the young, the new, the re-establishment and eternal re-generation of life and death as the cosmoses spin and mutually maintain. So, the cycle goes on.

But the symbolism has a deeper resonance: the spinning of the dreidel, its sides polarised between the All and the Nothing evokes the primal spin which brings Creation into being in our contemporary narrative of the Big Bang. Scientists tell us that from Nothing, the quantum vacuum, arises a Singularity which contains All. And time passes, and as it passes there are various processes of receiving and transforming, initiating and repeating, expanding and contracting as matter begins to form and cohere into the universe.

The moment of arising of All from Nothing is about as holy as it is possible to conceive. It is the Temple at the dawn of creation, the quantum moment, the supreme event. We are born and die as its children. I stood at the bedside of a man who knew this reality, and who was struggling right to the end to transmit his Knowing.

The actual moment Glyn left the earth had an impact which was noted by many of those who knew him. I reproduce here my own account written at the time:

'With a few others, I had been for hours by the deathbed of this man who had shaped our lives in Inner Work for thirty years; by guiding, challenging, opening worlds and landscapes of the Beyond, and making manifest to all who might be interested the intricate order of the invisible, the laws of the intangible. About 2 am, my husband and I left.

On returning late from the Hospice on that Monday morning, I found sleep impossible. But I must have fallen into a light doze, because suddenly I was seemingly pummelled awake by a pounding on my back, and rose up in confusion: *What? What? Is he gone?*

I lay awhile and then:

> *I saw two massive Gates in verdigris (the grey-green of old bronze) which were opening slowly. To the clanging of chains was added the deep rumble of big wheels, of processional wagon and casket, as if bearing a great warrior home to his rest. As the procession passed through the Gates, two vast angels of verdigris raised their trumpets high. The gates slowly closed, and the wheels rumbled away to Eternity.*

I wept, and fell into another light doze, but suddenly was awake again. I looked at the clock: exactly a quarter to six. Just silence. Nothing.

Presently I got up and walked in the garden of a new day in early Spring.

A little later I saw my husband's face through the window when he heard the news on the phone. As he came into the garden to tell me, I was engulfed by a wave of sheer exultation, of overwhelming joy at such a passing. Only afterwards, the grief.

It had occurred, of course, at a quarter to six.

Chapter 12

Initiation

The value of initiations. Some thoughts about the future of religion, myth and metaphysics.

I waited with considerable apprehension in a room in a strange house somewhere in the Midlands with a group of other women. We knew it was some kind of initiation, organised by the men, so it was mostly in silence that we watched one woman after another conducted from the room. When my turn came, I was led to a bathroom where there was a simple shift draped over a chair and a bath full of water. I was invited to take a quick bath and put on the shift and blindfold beside it, then knock on the door when I was ready.

I stripped, plunged into the bath, and gasped out loud. It was icy cold with a few ice-cubes floating in it. I needed no urging to be quick! After towelling myself dry, I donned the shift and blindfold and stood trembling at the door, every sense alert, braced, all my personal defences and pride geared to acquit myself well whatever ordeal lay ahead. I would rise to the challenge…

But my defences were no match for what followed. The door opened, and both my hands were gently taken. I was led, blindfolded, into a warm hallway. In the background, softly, just at the edge of hearing, the words of a tender popular song wove in and out, like the wind soughing through pines. I was led gently, carefully, down halls, up and down stairs, around and through, until I lost all sense of place and time. The house seemed enormous, but I must have been conducted through the same spaces. Always the soft warmth and the song drifting, and my hands held, guided, until every defence I had mustered dropped in shards, and I stood and walked above all emotion. I remember noting the way my emotions and all I had been, were swirling somewhere round my feet with the music. I was literally (in feeling) somewhere well 'above', clear and utterly secure.

After an eternity, I was guided into a room and the door closed behind me. Tenderly I felt my guide raise and kiss both my hands in a gesture which sent another shock of the unfamiliar through my stripped-down system. He departed and others led me to a chair, throne-like, on a dais. Then the blindfold was removed.

I was enthroned in semi-darkness and in the brightness at the other end of the room, which seemed very far away, stood four male figures. One was clad in roman armour as a warrior, one in the robes of a classical scholar, one a king and one a priest.

If I had been 'above' before, at this point I went back to the beginning of creation. I felt the joining of the two great primal forces, and indeed, I summoned Him, the Other, the Counterpart. As Great Mother I looked at the tiny male archetypal figures far down at the end of the room and realised I had given birth to them all, all the men of all the ages, and the whole human race with all its variety and colour streamed past me and vanished like smoke over to the right-hand side.

Time started again only when I stood and was led, disoriented, out of the room and into another where I saw my clothes neatly piled and waiting for me. I was left alone to come back down to earth, a new being.

We all gathered for a drink afterwards, and the women looked shaken, unfamiliar, but generally glowing. It was a beautifully conceived and executed initiation, and illustrates the power of a genuine initiation to produce a change of state and raise (or deepen) experience. The effects may last a long time, or be forgotten; nothing is automatically *conferred.*

Initiation

Initiation is usually understood as conferring some status on a person, or marking elevation in some hierarchy, or being admitted into a group. Glyn's understanding of initiation was none of these. He returned to the original meaning of the word, *to begin*, making it very clear that an initiation was a confirmation, not a bestowal of anything. It makes real what is there already, confirms it, and begins its potential activation. But afterwards it is up to the individual to make something of that beginning and integrate it into living and being. The psychological value of initiation is a formal acknowledgement of potential and a little impetus towards its realisation.

I only realised after his death, that Glyn had trained us in an Initiatic tradition. I had never considered them all together, the various interesting and specific formal occasions in which I had participated through the years. When he set something up, in order to establish some power for it, people were 'initiated' by a small ceremony, carefully designed to trigger the appropriate psycho-logic.

Magical initiations work the same way, as do religious sacraments (or as they *could*, if viewed as more than a habitual formality or custom). It is best if the initiate is prepared, perhaps by a little tension or effort, e.g., formally requested to present themselves at a particular time and place without any explanation as to why. The element of trust is important, so of course it must be in a context one is sure of, but to let go of preconceptions and self-protective shields, a little shock is valuable. The shock of that icy bath on body and mind completely reformatted my internal disc, everything extraneous wiped, and my shields visible even to me, the watching core within. Then it only took a gentle 'tap' for the remaining layers to fall. Effectiveness depends on how skilfully the symbolic actions are set up, the sequence, the symbols, the timing, and the coherency of the principles behind.

In a good ritual everything is chosen to evoke resonances which speak to the deeper psyche. For example, the raised chair evoked the throne imagery of the highest feminine principle Binah from the Kabbalah, and the Egyptian Goddess Isis, whose name which means 'seat or throne'. The way it is conducted also dictates the effect. Those severe shamanic initiations one can read about involving brutality, terror, harshness and physical extremes will certainly raise energy and produce a change of state. If the circumstances are in a stable context, punitive initiations may produce lasting change, with new psychic faculties becoming available. But that was not the way we did things, nor what was aimed at. *"Horses for courses,"* Glyn might say. Results can be gross or subtle.

Another well-respected form of initiation occurs in Guru traditions. I recently read an example of this which makes this point, and also another point perhaps relevant to Glyn. I read of an Indian master[1] who had in younger years earnestly acquired some books of philosophy but had to put them aside because he couldn't understand any of them. Within two months of his initiation by his Guru, which was a dramatic and life-changing event though only conveyed through words, he was expounding the philosophy in them to others. The Knowledge just happened effortlessly. I always felt that Glyn's erudition was not solely the product of learning: he had had no formal education or study, and he seemed to know a great deal more about everything than the rest of us with degrees aplenty! It's a phenomenon.

In parallel to the women, the men also underwent an initiation arranged by women. I wasn't involved with this, but heard some details after, and was struck by how different it was from ours. Kindness and courtesy had been a challenging factor for some of the women, including myself because of confounding expectations. One feisty woman had said after hers: "I just bawled at the end when they left me alone. I can cope with any kind of toughness, but if someone is kind to me, I go to pieces!" But the men were challenged in a different way. Although not confronted with anything threatening, each man had to make choices aimed at throwing something of his own nature into relief, and for some it was an ordeal.

The initiation element shakes up and tunes the whole psychological system, unlike an ideology or philosophy which may simply remain a system of ideas, however passionately espoused. In that sense our training was religious, and although it was compatible with a deeper understanding of conventional religious practice, most of the people drawn to Glyn's approach were looking for something which answered their religious urge in a re-visioned way, and to be enabled to bring new understanding to their religion of birth or choice. Leaving aside all the rigid features of institutional socio-political, custom-based mass religion so scorned by atheists, *religion at its best could be characterized as an organizer of emotional energy.* Ideally, it offers an organization of life based on the heart and aspirational values.

Ideally too, it *should* be a repository of wisdom. Wisdom does not arise through thinking alone, but by 'tasting' (sapere: to taste; be wise), experiencing, and it implies emotional maturity. Wisdom in itself is independent of religion, but the deeper values and inner training sheltering in the heart of the great religious traditions is likely to be the only firm ground on which to confront the challenge of the future, and in particular the question: where next with religion?

The Future

Historically, psychologically and socially the religious/spiritual is such an essential strand in human nature that I don't expect religion and religious expression ever to be subsumed into secularism, as some progressivists might anticipate, and old-time Marxists once confidently predicted. Cracks just show up in different places! From no culture in human history are religion and religious aspiration absent, and neither is it absent from modern secular global culture. The impulse to reach beyond oneself has simply morphed into less transcendent forms.

For instance, while it is important to resist wilful toxic pollution, malpractice and despoiling the environment, ecological concerns can acquire a kind of 'religious' authority for some. Likewise, football, political nationalism and terrorism can engage the fervour of quasi-religion, adding to the confused picture and immature understanding of religion in both public and private debate.

All too often in the media, for instance, religious discussion seems stuck at the level of an adolescent mix of pious platitudes, unexamined opinion and superficiality, lagging well behind the intelligence applied to other subjects, and not salvaged by the contribution of some religious professionals. As a result, religion in public discourse is merely politicized, sociologized or becomes a straw-man simplification which is easy to ridicule and reject for its human failings, and the metaphysical crisis seems as deep within institutional religion as it is in secular or humanist society.

It should be clear, even to the fiercest critic, that the political, social, cultural aspects of religion, its *material* manifestations, are not the whole of it. To debate religion without taking account of, and understanding the immaterial basis of it, is not *rational.* Faith, the religious impulse, is too deep, universal and manifestly essential to human nature to be reasoned away, and the future calls for an intelligent approach to the whole phenomenon. Mature and educated metaphysical awareness, in response to the evident 'crisis of meaning', will be our best hope of new avenues to channel religious experience. I believe this is what we should be striving towards, a form of cognition, neither pure intellect nor passionate emotion, which extends the boundaries of our worldview—personally and collectively.

Work in progress for most of us! The future of religion will have to take account of man 'playing god' and manipulating and extending the physical universe through space exploration, quantum dynamics and molecular advances. How does this fit with the traditional idea of 'God'? Are there limits to increasing human power, or should we be imposing them? What is happening in Psyche with all this god-like power and choice: self-inflation, terror, overwhelm? These deeply negative states are increasingly evident in people of all ages, and are characteristic of the absence of a meaningful foundation for living.

Identity is clearly an issue which is troubling many, as previously secure roles and categories break down into a sort of protoplasm of relativism. Morality needs a firm foundation. Without an intellectually and emotionally coherent overall framework such as was traditionally provided by a religious worldview (not the same thing as dogmatism or worldly power), the toxins of insecurity and fear can spread unchecked. A human being scared of being human (the mindset 'we are the most destructive animal on earth' etc.) is easy prey to the apparent security of materiality and dogma.

One step towards a more positive future is taken by resisting this descent into fear and negativity in our personal outlook, tempting though it is to go with the prevalent flow of despair and nihilism in conversation with friends. There is always a bigger view. The kind of feeding-frenzy of fright-scenarios generated in contemporary media is guaranteed to increase insecurities, and ironically therefore, dogmatism—every kind of dogmatism, including the safety of highly intolerant 'solutions'.

The next step would be to find a way to embrace the unknown-ness of the future, and ask the old perennial questions as if our life depends on them: *Why are we here? What's it all about? Who am 'I'?*

Micro and macro myth

Answers to these age-old questions are expressed in sacred mythology as a corpus of symbolic, metaphorical stories. The mythological overlap with actual history is often slight, but provides a fertile soil for earnest academics determined to excavate what is considered 'real' (ie. historical), or desperate for a new thesis topic or angle. However, true myth is a framework for preserving and passing on essential values and reminding about numinous experience. It is a condensed structure with several levels of analogy behind the surface of narrative or image, and communicates several densities of meaning simultaneously. Stories of gods, goddesses, heroes, the traversing of seas and deserts, voyages, quests, chalices, crosses, lotuses and the power of three-ness, sevens etc. are a tiny part of the universal lexicon of myth.

We need sacred myth just as much today as ever. Perhaps even more so, because we lack a pan-global language which resonates with the soul. So where can we look for narratives like this? We could start with the one undeniable expression of human creativity: technology. Technology has given us an extraordinary new vision of the wonder and beauty of nature on the micro-scale as well as the macro. With scientific investigation of the 'inner' environment, experiments in consciousness, parapsychology, and unexplainable healing incidents, it's no exaggeration to say that more questions than answers are arising every day. It is an excellent question-rich environment and time to be living in, and fits perfectly with the maxim: *Answers close doors; questions open them.*

On the macro scale we have dramatic new imagery of our galactic environment courtesy of the Hubble telescope, and from little sensory entities speeding their way out of the solar-system, forever entangled with us even when their eyes and voices have grown silent. These are seeds of myth, and also of soul. The galaxy has become part of our geography, and entered our psycho-sphere. On the macro-scale this is an identity shift, a seismic shift in our sense of self and place in the scheme of things. There is a real possibility of other conscious beings besides us in our galactic community, and potentially of communication with them, which would shatter every parochial assumption we've ever had. A change of perspective is a powerful tool.

In the fifties and sixties good science-fiction writing was in its hey-day. It was inspirational and mythic because the best writing was distinguished by visionary content and broad-scale scenarios exploring philosophical and psychological issues in the context of speculating about the nature and functioning of other conscious beings on other worlds. What would we share in consciousness, how might we differ, with what would we need to identify in order to understand each other? Such metaphysical and religious issues were examined in Sci-Fi as they played out through imagined futures, constituting a mythic education and probably preparatory conditioning for what may come. Even Star Wars hit the spot.

We human beings may need to adapt to widely variant and presently unknown conditions, and be confident in our identity in face of identities formed from very different conditioning. There is an old Hermetic esoteric principle *'As above, so below'* which states that there is a principle of correspondence in which the greater scale is reflected in similar laws of operation on the lesser. So for example, simple principles like one, three, two etc. inter-relate at all levels of creation, and as well as in Great Nature, are identifiable in the micro-cosmos of a conscious Being's psychology and physiology. Therefore, the same may well apply to any conscious being anywhere in the oneness of our uni-verse, and give us a starting point for mutual understanding. The ground is consciousness.

The Conquest of Space

There is one powerful metaphor we all share: space. It is our chief limiting parameter. We can transcend Time in our imagination, but we remain trapped in the space of where we are, bounded by the fact that I am here and you are over there, perhaps ten thousand miles away. Technology allows me to talk to you, see you, but our spaces are separate. Even in the same room, my body is my boundary, and you are in your body space. Each object in the room is spatially distinct. We think in spatial categories, separating out our ideas, organising them in exactly the manner we organise objects in space. Just about every preposition in the English language is a spatial metaphor: 'in', 'on', 'at'. They are all spatial referents, though our concepts may be abstract, e.g. I am *on* time; I am *in* a state of anxiety. We divide our life into spaces and compartmentalise whenever possible. That way we keep control; keep things in order.

Space appears to be our nemesis and gives rise to the metaphor of an *inner* life and an *outer* life. What is meant by *inner*? It does not exist in any kind of physical space able to be located by the surgeon's knife. Neither is it bound by the body's space, nor that of the immediate environment. Using the 'inner' word is a reflection of our tendency to categorize spatially, when the reality is that Life is just Life, an inseparable oneness. We actually exist in a cosmos which is not bounded by the parameters we place upon it. This is the ancient teaching: '*As above, so below*', and it is also the transcendence of polarity by realizing a third point.

In terms of universal myth, we live in an Age when our awareness, our psycho-sphere, has been extended into Outer Space, and we have some new furniture in the shape of new images and information. The human quest to probe the galaxy and the environs of earth is a common mythology, and along with other technological advances as yet unseen, will unavoidably re-shape our non-visible cosmos: the human psyche. *The Guard is changing…*

Space is neither light nor dark. It negates polarization. Light as an analogy for consciousness, reflects the way light is visible only when it strikes an object, or there is a locatable source, or appears as particle. Awareness is held to be luminous in itself *when it is known*. Prior to knowing, it is in the opposite complementary state: a Dark Field of Unknowing from which all 'known' arises, the zero-point field or vacuum within which are the fluctuations and interactions which give rise to particles and consequently matter. The metaphor of space is a perfect metaphor, both empty and full of potency, both luminous and dark.

For humanity to mature and adapt to the challenges of the future, cope with change, and work through crises of self-image and identity, all our belief-systems come under the microscope. How can the perennial upwelling of Faith be expressed in new ways? From the creative darkness of the human soul, what new sacred truth may arise with the force to capture the attention and love of modern man? What kind of fuel facilitates such a leap into the Unknown where a new God might wait?[2]

By 'new God' of course I mean new clothing, new imagery, new approach, new understanding. It is a transferred epithet: how could God ever be 'new'? Or more accurately, how could God ever not be new?

So, what's with 'God'? I don't use the word much, and neither did Glyn, who would speak of the One in preference. Theistic traditions utilise god-words confidently and assertively, but for me the name is unimportant. You cannot sit on the word 'chair', but there is an object which the word references, and in a lot of different shapes and sizes. Forty years after I set out on a determined quest to 'know God', what do I know?

Birth of the New

Glyn wasn't interested in a cogent lot of theory for its own sake: he wanted to make it real, to embed it in people as practical wisdom, as a practical philosophy and strategy for the development of consciousness and knowledge. At the end of his life I think he looked back on an interesting experiment, with some successes and some failures. He was quite open about those things he regarded as failing. "I've made mistakes," he said.

His legacy was two-fold. On the one hand is his detailed drawing forth and re-expression of Law—cosmic, universal laws—which although abstract and needing effort to elucidate, are preserved for posterity in number and line.[3] On the other, he instituted a way of working, which I've attempted to characterize and present through my descriptions and attitude throughout these writings. My personal approach, and my 'motivation' in the technical sense Glyn used it, may differ in some respects from his, and there is filtering through my own lens. However, that is quite in order. "We are generalists" he would repeat, and this meant that, unlike many other ways of working which attract people primarily with the same motivational drive and leads to a certain homogeneity in the group, the people Glyn drew to him were diverse, and working together was a part of the learning platform. It is fitting for a pattern known as the 'Fourth Way' to work in the world as it is. Since his passing, the work continues through individuals and small groups which continue to meet, and to develop and pass on the legacy of the training in whatever way as individuals they are equipped to do.

In the early days, Glyn gave lots of suggestions on the issue of women and female religious unfolding in response to my own preoccupation with feminine drives and potential. As a man he claimed not to really know about women, but his grasp of human psychology was such that his advicc and analysis was often spot-on. However, I didn't put some of his suggestions into actual practice because they felt slightly odd, both for myself, and to introduce into the collective we had established. Only now do I realise why, and that there was a stage needed before I, at any rate, was ready for them. The evidence bears out a devotional predilection among women; for example, the tradition of setting up a shrine in the home, but at that time I wouldn't have known what to put on any shrine. It was still a waiting game for me. No new form of 'the One' had cohered yet in any form which spoke to my soul.

There is an important issue here concerning the role of the feminine as the vessel for that cosmic birth, familiar, of course, from Marian imagery in Christianity, but in every other traditional symbolism as well. There is plenty of mythological precedent also for women as the generators and bestowers of power: Shakti /Kali myths, Isis, Demeter and the esoteric tradition of women as initiators of priests, particularly concerned with awakening seership. Seership includes the prophetic, mantic and intuitive skills which give form and clarity to what is inchoate. Glyn intimated that he saw women as having a special role in '*giving birth to the star, to that innate luminosity which can be born internally and go forth into the world*'. His words.

This internal birth relies on certain conditions. The 13th century mystic Meister Eckhart says "We are all meant to be mothers of God." It takes place in the midst of silence, in the very ground of the soul when, without image and without understanding, "a secret word" is spoken. It is the same mechanism as the "voice from the darkness".

In the Taoist meditational classic *The Secret of the Golden Flower*, similar instructions describe the concentration needed for the Light to circulate, so that a "seed" is formed in the stillness, in non-being in the middle of being. With time the powers of heaven and earth (light and dark) crystallize into the seed-pearl of a new body. It is analogous to the embrace of man and woman.

Psyche

Every spiritual teaching distinguishes a state of higher identity from that normal identification with what we know as 'I/me'. This greater identity embraces all the potentiality from which newness can be born, but is only known in mind-silence. We named the greater identity simply 'Psyche', meaning the totality of the individuality including that which is unconscious, as opposed to 'I', the organizational principle of personal ego. The powerful 'blowing away' effect sometimes produced by Glyn's presence was a result of encountering the level of Psyche operating through him, as it does in great teachers, saints and sages, and the effect is a temporary plunge into one's own silent Psyche where the chattering mind is still. At times, a different 'self' takes over, or is quietly watching in the background. For instance, the spontaneous 'slippages' which used to surprise me were a level of Psyche spontaneously taking the reins, albeit briefly, but with the value of simply in making me aware. And when I shifted 'above' during the initiation I have described, it was my Psyche who gazed across time and space. The experience and taste had a lasting impact, as it was designed to do.

A further example from my own life occurred under the stress of giving birth to my son. As the waves of contractions intensified, suddenly I slipped beyond them, humming lines from the Brahms German Requiem like a mantra: "Behold all flesh is as the grass, and all the glory of man is as the grasses blooming". I think it was the pulsating rhythm which carried me, but the words also have certain relevance at a moment of birth! Afterwards my husband commented that he had watched the contractions growing stronger on the monitor and wondered why I went quiet and began to smile peacefully. Although I could feel the contractions happening in my body, I was not *with* them. I was in some fields of Somewhere, watching...

Another time I screamed for help when the fingers of one hand were crushed between the frames of an old window which descended like a guillotine. Since it took some time and effort for help to arrive and manage to lever up the window to free them, I separated myself from the pain and waited patiently. The pain was in the fingers; I was not in the fingers. Why suffer?

Can we sustain and live from that greater 'I' which is, or can be, in communion with the Highest? Living, acting, speaking from interior silence, or 'basic nature' according to the necessity of the moment, is a permanent state some few attain, but it is a state both natural and fundamental to humanity. I was given another glimpse of the possibility as a result of sustained work on a particular course, when I felt 'myself' literally split into two. One was the normal slightly daft person solemnly in pursuit of an objective while chattering to herself; the other a dark silent one who watched with some amusement as the silly one rounded the side of the house looking for some object on the lawn. The silent one knew perfectly well it would not be found, and simply observed the antics with interest. So, who was I? The silent one, the chattering one, or one seeing both?

"Where will you be when your One has passed away?" Glyn's words in the Book of Jubilee.[4] A well-known Zen koan asks the same question, or rather, a different question with the same answer: "What was your original face before your parents were born?" The answer can't be spoken but can be known.

On his deathbed Glyn kept hold of some ping-pong balls stuck together in a tetrahedron which leaves a little gap in the centre where the four balls touch. This is the centre—in this gap, in Nothing. Each of the balls represents a different viewpoint. He had previously constructed similar models of icosahedron and dodecahedron, elasticated so the centre balls could be shifted. He studied these intensively, and the implications of how *views are determined by the place from which one stands to look.* I was intrigued that these little white balls were his last possession, as if they were a key to the worlds beyond. After death, I placed them beside his head as he lay in stillness.

The birth of a new vision of the Divine reality can only arise from Knowledge, not from the self-serving pre-occupations of the associative mind driving normal ego. *"The old order is changing"*, Glyn had said cryptically. I didn't really know what he meant, but I trusted that anything we did to elucidate the underlying Laws of it all would contribute in a small way to the new Order.

Worm-Dragon-Angel

In an attempt to put some mythological form on his abstract philosophy and diagrams, late in his teaching life Glyn put together a London seminar series based on the imagery of Worm-Dragon-Angel. Over twelve weeks, the seminar linked together a complex hierarchy of octaves depicting the inter-relationship in human being of *worm-function, dragon-energy and angel-clarity.*

The worm is our basic nature and physical functioning. The ancient symbol of a dragon is an image of sheer energy, sometimes positive, sometimes negative; sometimes worm-like, sometimes winged. When mass energy takes hold of people's emotional being and generates violence and bloodshed, it is like a rampaging fire-breathing dragon. Fashions, enthusiasms, causes and compulsions can be dragons, useful if tamed and ridden, destructive if out of hand, and they very easily get out of hand because of the energy and emotion involved. However, by commanding the dragon of one's own nature, the energy can enable the creation of new *Dragonways* for others, and the passing on of methods to tame and utilize dragon energy.

A new Order has to arise from the *Worm* or serpent of our basic nature, grow through the *Dragon* controlled and directed, and shine as the *Angel* in a new City of Earth, with a new Temple at is heart. This mythological vision isn't just a vision of the future, but recognition of work to be done now, by each of us committed to the quest for Knowledge.

So, in steps and stages, haltingly, through dark periods and light, through words, image, action, through intention and persistence, I have pursued the intimation I nursed long ago as a child, when I would sit for hours on a cliff-edge hollowed from the dusty Australian soil, watching the evening settling over the ocean, and keeping a watchful eye out for aggressive bull-ants approaching my bottom.

I'm grateful to have encountered a phenomenon like Glyn. Glyns arise here and there, regularly I suspect, and often unknown, unless the cog-wheels of history need to throw someone on to the world-stage. Without these manifestations, we would have long forgotten, as a race, where we have come from, and what our potential is.

All is within Unity. All my faltering words, my maladroit presentation of a work-experience involving many people and many ideas I have not even attempted to do justice to—all these are within Unity. The One God within each of us is an individual responsibility to seek out and make real. As a race I hope we will discern a new face of God in the ages to come. We'll all see differently, of course, and fight, but none of these viewpoints will make the slightest difference to the reality, or to the potential for each of us to find the One within.

As for love, it's not quite what I thought when I started out on the path.

When Love is compared to a flame, to fire in the heart, the analogy overlooks the fact that fire always needs to consume something. When the oil is consumed, or the wood reduced to ash, the flame goes out. When a sacred lamp is steady and burning in the darkness, it needs controlled conditions and fuel to maintain its steadiness.

The fuel, and the keeping of the flame, is at the heart of this book.

---

1. *Beyond Freedom, Talks with Sri Nisargadatta Maharaj*, ed Jory P.402
2. See Prologue. Letters of an Amnesiac
3. see http://www.sareoso.org/

Epilogue

Readers might be asking 'Where can I go to pursue this kind of approach to inner work?'

Like seeds, all the practical skills and abstract principles I have presented are transferable to any place and mode of life in which you find yourself. You have to grow them yourself in your own ground, starting where you are, and with what you come across. It's more than helpful to share with others, even if you have to set up the context of exploration yourself. For example, any *traditional structured* teaching is an explanation of something, and can be worked with. What does it actually *mean*? The seed of truth may lurk under layers of sacerdotal interpretations, well-worn images or elaborations accumulated down the ages. It may only be a seed, but if you scrape off the dirt you can plant this kernel.

Ironically the hardest shells to penetrate are those most familiar to us: the well-worn dogmas of our upbringing, both religious and secular. Once-living truths get pulverised into pabulum by the grinders of custom and repetition. However, it is possible to look for the common ground in spiritual paths—not the clothing in symbol, imagery, or customs—but at the origin and essence, where these abstract entities called *principles* can be found. True principles are based on experience, but are not the same as experiencing *states*, heightened or otherwise, despite the dominance of this aspiration in much spirituality. Principles condition behaviour, attitude and expectation as well as providing a way of seeing further, making it possible to dig beneath the surface, not just re-arrange ideas. I have tried to give a practical illustration through the narrative itself.

The difference between some contemporary methods and the path I have presented in this book, is training. An esoteric path may seem almost perversely tough and effortful, but its aim is not sudden and radical insights or personal happiness, but Knowledge with a foundation strong and clear enough to be passed on to others and down the generations.

The point is that if you know the steps, a method can be passed on. Being told *about* the goal won't cut it. There are many paths up a mountain, but although the view at the top might be spectacular, no true mountaineer wants to be dropped from a helicopter at the summit for a brief look. How much beauty and knowledge would be missed on the way, plus there's always the risk that the effortless vision of glory is obscured by cloud for the entire time at the summit!

Knowledge advances civilisation. Without the philosophy and formulation of those who have gone before we would not have the art and culture of our heritage. The education of human Being is a process, a passing-on, an uncovering of the laws of continuous generation. Glyn was looking ahead—at least four hundred years ahead, he regularly said, though why four hundred is unclear. He utilised always the most straightforward labels and explanations, neutral language and philosophical principles stripped to their base in number, precisely so that the understanding of them could be transferred to different contexts and be preserved into the future.

'We', the nameless colleagues of my narrative with whom I shared these many years of working, are still working with the legacy Glyn left. When the Association under the name Saros was dissolved, there was no longer an institution to absorb all the energy into its own identity and maintenance, but the energy of its Foundation still exists, and individuals have taken different paths to anchor the teaching in their own spheres of expertise. Some group activities still take place in various areas mostly in England, but with some individuals scattered in other parts of the world. The love generated by shared depths, wonder and suffering, and by a shared calling to the magnetic centre of Glyn in life and death, still exists. Without all these Friends in the Work, it would not have been possible.

So, dear reader, in the terrifying exuberance of the Global village, with an explosion of options and no firm signage for you in particular to follow, look to what is around you and select the best. Discriminate; try to discern the gold within a tradition or teaching, which will ultimately be discerned by how closely it conforms to the fundamental principles of the cosmos, not in charismatic ideas. Gold may be found through literature, in symbolism, in humble action, and some may even speak it, but words of genuine value spring from deep roots. The old principle of trusting to Necessity, God or the Universe to provide, still holds true. Faith is perennial.

All the guidelines I presented in Chapter 5 will be fruitful in any context. '*Neither accept, nor reject*' is a useful modus operandi for all internal work, along with '*No criticism, even of oneself*'. Otherwise you may close doors before you have opened them properly.

And then—work in the life around you, in the life which is yours, and the circumstances which have arisen for you to hoe your furrow and grow the grain you have been given.

When that grain has ripened, when fuel has been collected and distilled for your own journey by wonder, suffering and far-sight, you may encounter a magnetic centre, a galactic centre, a supreme event, whether it be for a moment or a lifetime, and *Know*.

I take my leave and wish you well, and hope that you too may find Friends in the Work.

Glyn should have the last word:

The birds from the trees upon the hill
announce, as they will and have since
they began to sing, the new millennia.

For what is new is only old tempered
by wind of changing circumstance.

Cry Jubilee unheard: the Lord shall
hear your song and speak it to the
wind. The birds will sing it then as now.[1]

---

1. The Book of Jubilee, Cranswick Press 1984

* Author's website: www.meaningbydesign.co.uk

Postlude

WORM – DRAGON – ANGEL

In verse form, an evocation of three levels of the emotional drive within the Psyche. There are parallels with more traditional mythic imagery, and it is a developmental hierarchy.

SONG OF THE WORM

The worm turns and tunnels
Questing, seeking, twisting
In the dark encoiling tubes
Of the mind of Man.
Open, earth. Open, hidden heavy
Molecules of matter.
Open, ways of knowledge.
Give me food to grow,
Light to see in dark complexity.
Give me things, people, places
To investigate, to note, to experience,
For I am a worm with attitude
And I need to grow, to know, to hoe
The furrows of the universe.
Give me books to gnaw,
And screens to bug,
And any kind of information
For my greedy maw.

Give me more of anything.
I need, indeed, to know.

LAY OF THE DRAGON

What noble beast of claw and wing!
I sleep with the worm
But wake with the dawn
Of wormly admiration,
And how I love to love
when I burst into the day!
I ride the tides of men,
Waxing when the heart swells
And surfing the currents of the feeling mind.
Feed me with art and music,
Tickle my scales with poetic fancy,
But stand back when I gather to a force
And carry all before me,
Sounding the drums of passion
For a multitude of causes.
To know me, you have to take a stand
And clear a way
To the end of the earth
And the beginning of time.
I cannot be known without stillness,
When the heart stops, the breath holds,
And the mind lies full and calm
Upon the straits of love.
This knowledge is a treasure,
A trove, by Jove.

ROUND OF THE ANGEL

Where am I ?
Knock at the gate,
Penetrate the riddle
Of the sands of time,
And I am known and Knower
At the crossroads of eternity.
To maintain vision of the angel
You must work like an elephant
And labour like a mule,
And wrest the secret from the bricks of life
By sheer determination.
Do not scorn dirt on your hands,
Or laughter in your face,
And infiltrate the guts of circumstance
With delicacy of mind and clarity of heart.
My food is nothing, and everything.
When you are the One,
And the world is the Other,
The worm turns, the dragon wakes,
The angel streams through every gap and crevice
Of the brute and stony ground
Of being and creation.
Don't look up. Or down.
My way is poised on the head of a pin.
I put the ledge in knowledge;
This, Man, you'd better believe!

Appendix I

This diagram illustrates how 3 simple forces (the axes Affirming, Denying, Unifying) combine into 6 Orders of Action, Constructors of the universe.

Imagine a force following a direction. It meets a second force and is turned in its direction, and then encounters the third and is turned again which creates a sort of swirling balance of the three constituent forces. The names of the six resulting Constructors reflect the ordering within them, as forces which expand, repeat, contract, receive, transform, initiate all things.

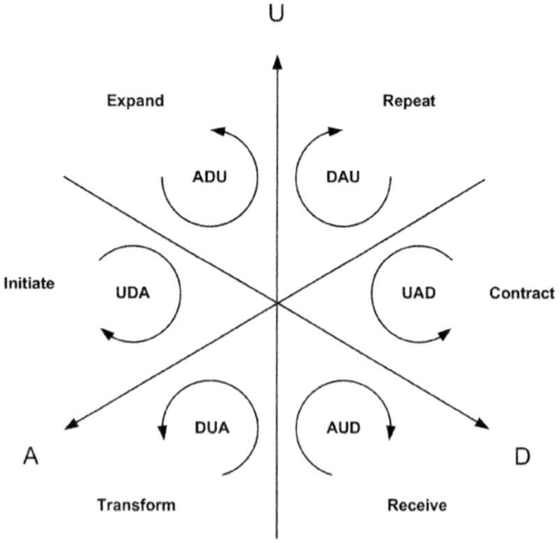

If you place them as six points in a circle, and connect with a single line without any repetition, only 12 shapes are possible from six. See them as any set of 12 identities, conditioned and named according to context.

Appendix I

TWELVE SIGILS

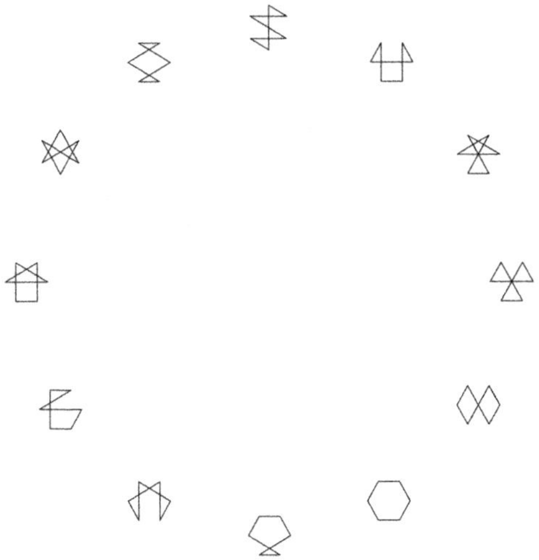

THE DOUBLE DIAMOND or HUMAN OCTAVE
(Chapter 7)

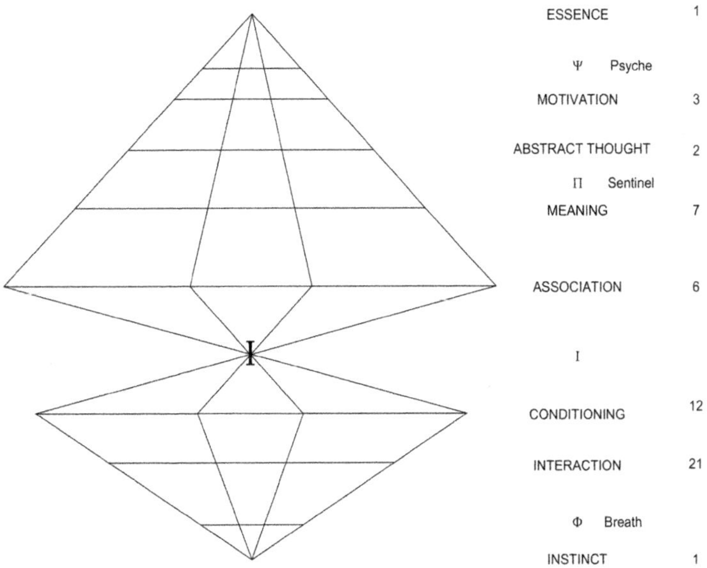

OCTAVE OF CREATION

This shows how the Human Octave fills the interval between six and twelve on the Great Octave, providing the conscious energy needed for creation to proceed.

	0				
Do	1	Will			
Si	3	Mothers			
La	2	Gate			
So	7	Temple			
Fa	6	Constructors	1	Essence	
					Ψ Psyche
			3	Motivation	
			2	Abstract Thought	
					Π Sentinel
			7	Meaning	
			6	Association	
					I
			12	Conditioning	
			21	Interaction	
					Φ Breath
Mi	12	Identities	1	Instinct	
Re	21	Governances			
Do	1	Oneness			

Diagrams courtesy of Michael Frenda.

Appendix II: Twelve Aphorisms

The mind is without form,
and the spirit of the Divine hovers over its waters,
and darkness is upon its depth.

In the beginning is the Word
and the Word is with God
and the Word is God.

The One giveth and the One taketh away.
Blessed be the Name of the One.

Affirm Unity within, Unity without.
It is not mocked, it is not broken, does and does not exist, has no qualities, no time or space, no substance.
Affirm Unity.
Unity, Unity, Unity.

Pick fruit and pass it on. The same is a service.
Pick fruit and eat it: you will be asked to account for it.

The dead do not praise God,
neither do they who go down into silence.

Seek permanence, seek the Mother.
Seek impermanence, seek the Father.
Seek the Void, seek to end existence.
These three bind consciousness to form.

Where were you when the worlds began?
Where are you now?
Where shall you be when your One has passed away?

That mind which is the hidden wisdom lies still and tranquil
like good wine resting in the cask.

At the height and the depth of the well of Knowledge,
draw from the unlnown into the known,
and know that the deep remains unknown.

Seek the singer not the song.
The singer remains when the song has gone.

The Lord is in his holy temple.
Let all the world keep silence before him.

All these aphorisms are beautifully translated into a Script devised from the meditation system.
http://www.highpeakmeditation.org.uk/aphorisms.htm
Here is the first:

The mind is without form

and ters

the wa

spirit its

of the over

divine hovers

AND DARKNESS IS UPON ITS DEPTH

Appendix III

Complete versions of original poems quoted in the text

THE LAST SUPPER – Leaving Melbourne

On that last night
were all the threads of our common lives
tied, and hung round my shoulders:
a lei to carry through the world.

I, the wanderer,
of your munificence grown and gone,
hatched like a turtle from the washing tide.
Another Last Supper, with tempered forms
strained to left and right of the candlelight,
the wit, the wine the Christ for a night.
And the turn of a head catching a lustre
of love surprised by leaving
the clinking together of years
on some great rolling silence.
We the young, have seeded together
and must bear fruit.
Did some buffoon plant hairy legs on table,
another wave elixir of the gods
so each leafy, gupping mouth streamed with emerald?
We will not die tonight,
and all the broad streets are warm with stars.

The summer wind was nudging at the sand
of that last night, shifting grain by grain.
Laissez.. Laissez... Je vais with the black sea
muttering far out into gaping lands:
the unforeseeable future, peopled with vast imagining
and doomed to diminution
through the sucking mouth of time.
Did I know then of pools which fill and form
like old liqueurs, encrusting the memory?
Pass the chartreuse, all gritty with salt,
in a bevy of friends, supped and supine on the beach.
I am leaving them, unquestioningly, unexplainable,
but moving with the pull of multiplicity
and the one-shot law of life.

Knotting every shared hour into one night,
when laughter grew ragged,
we left before the dawn.

GAZELLES

Your harness, Love, and the wheels of your power like suns
Will make of me a wide, wide pasture where gazelles from the desert
Can come and graze by night. And there the body's sea will rock
A respite from the waterless heart, the dry mounds moving,
The slipping sands that sabotage the crests of wind-razed thought…

They say when even wind withholds,
The dunes are heard to boom:
The desert ululates her daemon-lover.

In sleeping fields the dark-rimmed animals
Are listening, stepping lightly as the moon
To milk the faintest sounds within the earth.
There Love, you wait. I will bear
Your wingèd worm which makes the body bloom
Its heavy fruit, its slyly obsolescent opulence,
Until the living creatures come to rein,
And Earth and I, your minions, split like pods.

Love is fierce: an insemination spreading
Breast to breast.
And the shy-eyed herds are lustrous…

Lying down a woman, I rise a warrior.

DEATH AND MEDITATION

Around me, like a summer field of poppies
Lies the Feared,
The only-forgotten son of all our fathers,
The reaper and the reaped, the open maw
Which dogs the back of every waking lover,
The blind spot in the eye.

I acknowledge you, field of bright infinity;
Call you the crimson round the cup
Of every dark lost place of being,
The interstices of moments on the run.

Lover, look back. When the eye turns in
And the carnival stills,
Its music and horses fled to some summer
Moving in snatches on the rim, and are gone into time
Time is unwound and love is full.

TO MARS

Great War-god I salute you,
You Prodigal, you Lover in my arms!
I speak for all the wombs of the unborn;
Rank upon rank we wait,
Not to scavenge petals from the earth
Beneath your keening sword,
But in silence, to acknowledge by blood light
All beginnings, all life which spills itself
On the rocky desert floor,
That somewhere and everywhere
by a crumbling wall, a rampart of sand,
One other poppy may flower in the early sun.

REQUIEM FOR MY FATHER

Death will come with the night wind from the stars,
Treading softly, the universe in its wings,
And touching you will whisper 'Come'.
We shall rise up, you and I, and follow
Through the gate into a mighty plain.
No star shines here but one, enormously.
Bewildered, you alone must go into the light
To meet your destiny, while I remain
To honour you, my father, and point towards eternity.

THE MOTHERS

There came a time when destiny each day
out-folded full as the formal cream
of the first magnolia bloom on its skeleton stem,
while nearby a blackbird raped the last rotten berry
from long gone autumns and many frozen years.

There are many ways a woman can give birth
many ways of knowing woman and that fruition
her body has by rote and cannot understand,
for she is merely audience to her body's festival.
The manikin she dandles through its early years,
life-fodder, is beautiful as life, but when
the earth reclaims its own all dues are squared again.
Full creation is a change of quality:
that minute setting of the forms which brings
not increase of water, but over-abundantly,
rarely, evoking wonder, the crimson of wine.

I herald the fathers, givers of the waters.
He who first infused my timid flesh
cloying round an image of the moon afloat
with his own established light, with the rock
of his power and went his way undiminished.
He who gently warmed the snows that settled then
with fires and roasting nuts and laughter
and gave to green and growing things their space.
And he who came like a gale in March,
blasting round the roots, until the body stood
in defence of its inwardness, and when that wanton

expenditure of essence was past, bloomed and was full.

They go. A Father is forever taking leave.
Staying is the Mothers' sway, we riders of time,
reapers of the bounty fed out into space.
We who gain a hundred-fold at point of greatest loss
and discriminate, nurture the single into form.
But waiting has an end, and when all veils are lifted
She sees the long procession of the living,
And stands, and knows, and is Herself.

L.O